CYCLE PSYCHED

"*Cycle Psyched* helps identify the questions that make athletes into champions, along with practical answers to help you succeed, refine, or extend your competitive career."

—Phil Gaimon, Pro Veteran, Author

"Saul and Peg outline clearly and concisely what it takes mentally to compete at a world-class level. *Cycle Psyched* is a must-read for any athlete at any level."

—Leah Goldstein, RAAM Solo Champion

"*Cycle Psyched* is a solid mix of some excellent mental coaching and pro wisdom that can really strengthen your mental game. Check it out."

—Steve Bauer, Olympic and World Champion Medalist

"*Cycle Psyched* is a complete guide for any aspiring cyclists, to mentally prepare to achieve your goals. I especially like the practical advice, specific to cycling, with useful examples of how to apply it."

—Nicole Cooke, Olympic Road and Road World Champion

"*Cycle Psyched* is a good read with very practical advice that will help you to perform better as a cyclist… or at anything else you do. Trust me, the breathing and focusing techniques are empowering."

—Brian Walton, Olympic Medalist, Founder Walton Endurance

"A great read filled with wisdom from dozens of the world's top cyclists on strengthening your mind, sharpening your focus, and developing the emotional control to significantly improve your cycling. Strongly recommended for anyone pursuing the sport competitively at any level."

—Maggie Coles-Lyster, National Champion

"Whether you are racing traffic in New York City or other racers in the World Championship and Olympics, it's important to be fit and have a strong mental game. *Cycle Psyched* offers solid practical coaching and excellent professional advice on strengthening your mental game that will help you to race with more power, speed, and enjoyment."

—Nelson Vails, Olympic and World Champion Medalist

"I like the book and the exercises and homework. It validates some of what I already do, and I look forward to trying some intriguing new ideas, like sending energy out through my body like a five-pointed star. I can see myself using the ideas and exercises to prepare mentally."

—Clara Honsinger, National Cyclocross Champion

"As a coach, I really like the book. The tools and exercises provided for mental training are effective and easy for the athletes to understand and follow. For sure, when it comes to psychology and athletes learning mental skills, this book will make my job as a coach much easier."

—Houshang Amiri, Head Coach Pacific Cycling Centre

"Sports psychologist Saul Miller explores and explains the mental side of the world's hardest sport, cycling, in his new book *Cycle Psyched.* Doing a deep dive on humans' strongest muscle, our brains, he also explores the differences between us, and how these elite athletes can be motivated to achieve greatness. The interviews and testimonials from top cyclists are both entertaining, and provide behind-the-scenes insight into a subject that will be of interest to both cycling fans and others interested in sports performance. A fascinating, thoroughly enjoyable read."

—Sylvan Adams, Founder ISN, Masters Cycling Champion

"Peggy was a key member of our original 7-Eleven Women's Cycling Team. Teaming up with Sport Psychologist Dr. Saul Miller makes a formidable duo. In *Cycle Psyched* they present an outstanding strategy for improving any racers' mental game."

—Jim Ochowicz, Founder of Iconic 7-Eleven Cycling Team

PRO WISDOM
AND THE MENTAL
TRAINING TO EXCEL

CYCLE PSYCHED

Dr. Saul L. Miller & Peggy Maass Labiuk

SPRING CEDARS

First edition, 2023

Cover illustrations by Lauren Zurcher
Book and cover design by Spring Cedars

ISBN 978-1-950484-89-8 (paperback)
ISBN 978-1-950484-90-4 (ebook)

Published by Spring Cedars
Denver, Colorado
www.springcedars.com

CONTENTS

This book is dedicated to all the cyclists who love the speed, power, and freedom of this wonderful sport.

Afghan refugee and cyclist Shaima Nasiri, celebrating the joy of a sunset ride in liberty along the shores of Vancouver, B.C. In her escape from tyranny, Nasiri was aided by Sylvan Adams and others who love freedom and cycling.

INTRODUCTION

The science of training for bike racing is no longer a mystery. We can measure forces, heart rates, efficiency of oxygen uptake in the blood, and lactate thresholds, as well as time-honored speed, cadence, and distance. We know what physical and technical parameters must be met in order to produce winning cyclists in any discipline. However, one factor that hasn't been as regimented and is relatively neglected, is the training of the mind. Focus, commitment, belief, confidence, emotional control, and the ability to deal with fear, frustration, pain, and difficulty are critical factors in a cyclist's success…that's what *Cycle Psyched* is about.

CYCLE WISDOM

"There are so many facets to performance where psychology has an impact: setting goals, dealing with setbacks in training, managing priorities, and then getting to the start line ready to race with some tactical plans ready to use."

—Nicole Cooke, Great Britain, Olympic Road and Road World Champion[1]

CYCLE WISDOM

"In order to really perform in cycling you have to be able to push yourself real deep... and that comes from the mind. The body does the work and when the mind says, 'enough, stop,' you're done. The mind focuses the energy to perform, and if the mind lets go, performance is over."

—Steve Bauer, Canada, Olympic Road and Pro Road World Championships Medalist, UCI WorldTeam Directeur Sportif[2]

CYCLE WISDOM

"Mental preparation makes all the difference in the world between being a good rider and a rider who wins."

—Leonard Harvey Nitz, U.S.A., Olympic Track Medalist[3]

In *Cycle Psyched*, we provide the means to grow your mental strengths. Just as you train yourself physically to increase speed, strength, and endurance, and work to improve your cycling skills, following this mental training plan will improve your performance and enjoyment in the best activity on two wheels.

CYCLE WISDOM

"Basically, I think whether we win or lose is ultimately decided in our minds."

—Peter Sagan, Slovakia, 3x Pro Road World Champion[4]

Peter Sagan

Excellence in any sport is the result of the successful integration of physical, technical, and mental factors. While most athletes and coaches would agree that success in their sport is at least 50 percent mental, there is a disproportionate emphasis on the physical and technical aspects, and mental training may be underrated or neglected. But not by winners.

This book is a tool to help you train and develop the focus, feelings, and mental strength to improve your cycling performance and pleasure. Internationally renowned sport psychologist and author Dr. Saul L. Miller provides the mental coaching, and former world medalist, world record holder, National Champion, and cycling coach Peggy Maass Labiuk adds her experience.

In addition, the book contains insights and comments from over 90 of the world's top cyclists, including many who have raced and won stages in the ~3,500 kilometer, 21-stage Tour de France. Plus, there is input from numerous world and Olympic champions and medalists on the road, track, cyclocross, and mountain bike, as well as a solo winner of The Race Across America, an extreme, ultra-endurance, 4,800 kilometer challenge.

We encourage you to embrace the coaching provided and complete the exercises and homework as part of your training for success.

CHAPTER 1
The Three Keys

CYCLE WISDOM

"The real road race is not on the hot, paved roads, the torturous off-road curves, or the smooth-surfaced velodrome. It's is the electrochemical pathways of your mind."

—*Alexi Grewal, U.S.A., Olympic Road Race Gold Medalist*[5]

There are three key principles for managing your mind effectively:

1. **The first principle is that the mind is like an amazing, human super computer.** It's YOUR super computer. You are response-able to control the flow of thoughts and feelings. You are in charge. If what you are experiencing isn't positive, if it doesn't give you power or pleasure, shift to another program. Staying attentive and committed to running power programs on your mental super computer is a matter of choice, and it's a critically important part of developing a winning mindset.
2. **The second principle is that we get more of what we focus on.** The mental principle of lateral inhibition states that whatever we focus on becomes magnified in our perceptual field while all other stimuli are minimized. So if you are running negative, anxious, or frustrated thoughts or feelings, these programs will

inevitably lead to more tension, stress, and disease. A rider who thinks *this is too hard* or *I'm going to blow up, crash, or fail,* increases the probability of that happening. In contrast, if what you are experiencing is positive and empowering, something that gives you energy and inspiration, that programming will support you in creating more success and enjoyment on the road, track, or mountain…and in life. Okay, sounds pretty straightforward, but you may ask, "Why don't we create positive thoughts and feelings all the time?" It's because of the way our brains function.

3. **The third principle relates to the way we are hard-wired as human beings.** The way our nervous systems work is that our feelings affect our thinking, and our thinking affects our feelings. Every time you feel anxious, an anxious thought goes automatically with it, and vice versa.

Relationship of Thought and Feeling

SAUL: Along with being a sport psychologist, I used to run a pain clinic treating people who had been injured and were living with pain. If someone had a pain in their back, a thought would pop into their mind, such as, *I hurt*, or *be careful*, or *there's something wrong with me, I need some medication*, or *I'd better take it easy or lie down*. The specific thought doesn't matter; the important point to understand is that whenever there was a painful feeling, a cautious, tensing thought automatically went with it. It's the way we are wired. Similarly, if an athlete about to race is feeling anxious or nervous, thoughts that may accompany that angst are, *don't fail*, *don't mess up*, *don't crash*, and *be careful*.

PEGGY: I have many examples of this from my racing years. Lately, I have been experiencing those negative thoughts as I recover from a broken clavicle. When it hurts, I catch myself thinking *be careful, take it easy,* and I know that pattern could accompany me onto the bike when I start riding again…that is, until I take a breath and choose to shift my thinking, or until the pain eases.

SAUL: Sometimes we create circular thought-feeling loops that limit us. The thoughts and feelings that most frequently affect and limit cyclists have to do with fear, pain, and difficulty. The latter may take the form of not having the energy to challenge or persevere, or of feeling a sense of impossibility in relation to the difficult task at hand. The problem is these negative thoughts and feelings can produce more limited thinking, and more limited feelings, creating a negative loop that is like a trap. That is exactly how a slump develops. Negative feelings feed and produce negative thoughts which create and produce more negative feelings.

The feelings that most limit cyclists are thoughts of fear, pain, and difficulty.

Feeling	**Thought**
Fear (of failure)	*Don't make a mistake. Don't mess up.*
Fear (of injury)	*Be careful. Watch out. Be safe.*
Pain	*I hurt. It's too much. Be careful.*
Frustration	*No way. Not again. What's the use.*
Anger	*I'm going to get him/her. Get even.*
Fatigue	*I'm beat. Not now. I just can't.*

SAUL: In the 40 years I have consulted as a sport psychologist, I have observed three keys to having a winning mental game. These keys are interrelated and are the cornerstones of building mental strength. They are: Right Focus, Right Feeling, and Right Attitude.

Right Focus. Knowing who you are, what your goals are, and having a plan to achieve success. It's about supporting your goals with positive self-talk and high-performance imagery. Right Focus creates a positive, healthy, high-performance mindset. We get more of what we think about. This key is discussed in Chapters 2, 3, and 4.

Right Feeling. Creating and maintaining the feelings and emotions that will help you perform at your best. For some riders, that means feeling powerful, energized, and upbeat. For others, it's feeling more calm, centered, confident, and in control. Right Feeling also means not being distracted and limited by fear, anger, frustration, or pressure. Conscious Breathing is an essential element to creating and maintaining Right Feeling. This key is discussed in Chapters 5 and 6.

Right Attitude. A matter of choice. A winning, Cycle Psyched attitude is characterized by motivation, commitment, confidence, identity, and a love of cycling and the challenge it represents…plus living a lifestyle that supports both your competitive success and your well-being. This key is discussed in Chapters 7, 8, and 9.

RIGHT FOCUS

In this section (Chapters 2, 3, and 4), we discuss focus…what you consciously tune into on your mental super computer. You are the boss. You are response-able to run quality programs; that is, to create positive goals, thoughts, and high-performance images which will help you excel.

CHAPTER 2
Goals & Self-Assessment

Goals

Goals are the cornerstone of Right Focus. Let's review how to set helpful, meaningful goals.

SAUL: I'm a strong advocate of goal setting. It's important to know what you want to achieve and to have a plan to get there. There's a saying: A goal without a plan is just a wish. So set clear goals, shape the plan with long-term, intermediate, and short-term goals. Understand that how you talk to yourself as you work your goals is also very important. Goal setting is like planting a seed in your consciousness. Positive thinking nurtures that seed and supports it growing into something special. Negative thinking destroys it and undermines achievement.

What Are Your Goals? What is it you want to accomplish in cycling? Clear, meaningful goals are energizing and provide direction.

CYCLE WISDOM

"The most powerful thing you can do is set goals. The most important thing is the mind. That's where the power is, believing in your goals."

—Alison Sydor, Canada, Olympic Mountain Bike Cross-Country Medalist, Cross-Country World Champion, Road World Championship Medalist[6]

SAUL: After Leah Goldstein won the 2021 Race Across America, the first time in the 39-year history of RAAM that a woman won the overall solo category, I asked, what are the mental obstacles that challenge you?

LEAH GOLDSTEIN: RAAM is 3,000 miles. I can't stop and get off the bike, so I have to be calm and not panic. That's the biggest thing. You are going to be sore, and you go into these cycles where you feel like superman, then you feel terrible, then you feel like superman again. It's going to be repeated and repeated, and you have to know during these low times that it will pass…back off a bit and recoup, let your body recover, and don't panic. I think that's the biggest thing. When you are riding a 50 km TT, you can be thinking, *only 10 km to go*. Ultra-endurance requires a completely different mindset. You will get saddlesores that get infected, or your feet are swelling, and then your hands are swelling, all these different elements come up that didn't happen in the shorter races. And it's really your mental ability of learning to be comfortable while being uncomfortable, that's one of the biggest things, that makes the difference.

SAUL: In learning to be comfortable when you are uncomfortable, is there something you say to yourself, a mantra, that helps you manage the discomfort? A thought, like, *stay calm*?

LEAH GOLDSTEIN: Yes, you think about what your goal is and that everyone is in the same boat, and it really comes down to who can suffer the longest. You think about what this means to you. And what you've done to prepare for this, and how it's important to you, and why you are out there. When you put all that into perspective, what is clear is the regret you know you'll experience if you quit. Quit now, and you are going to regret it for the rest of your life. So I can be in pain for seven or eight days. I'm going to give it my best shot…. Yeah, you've got to think about how much you want it and the consequences of giving up.[7]

Leah Goldstein

Create **SMART** cycling goals: Specific, Measurable, Attainable, Relevant, Timely.

> **S**pecific
> E.g., a speed or time in a time trial or hill repeat, or qualifying for a specific event.
>
> **M**easurable
> Using a timed distance under similar conditions is best, rather than a place in the finishing order.
>
> **A**ttainable
> Specific time for the given distance or km/hr is attainable if you have been doing speed intervals or hill reps, and you are prepared for the effort.
>
> **R**elevant
> The goal should be meaningful to you and represent a significant positive achievement.
>
> **T**imely
> Set a specific and sensible timeline for achieving your cycling goal. If you are really committed to improving your cycling, write your goal down and read it to yourself periodically (it keeps it from fading away).

You can conceptualize your goals as a staircase with the long-term goals A at the top, intermediate goals B are what you need to do to position yourself to achieve A, and short-term goals C which support you in taking the steps to reach B.

A ________

B ________

C ________

Long-Term Goals

The most energizing goals are those that really mean something to you.

CYCLE WISDOM

"My dream was to become professional. But now I achieved that, so I need to set myself new dreams. Of course, Tour de France. When I started to cycle, I only knew about Tour de France actually. It was of course the dream to be at the Tour de France…or even win it!"

—Tadej Pogačar, Slovenia, Second Youngest Tour de France Winner, Youngest Tour of California Winner at Age 19[8]

Reflecting on his career, Phil Gaimon wrote:

> "So what's the point? Dream small? Dream reasonable? Don't dream at all? I'm glad my parents didn't encourage me to make cycling my profession, because if they had, boy would I be pissed now. I want to resent the old guys who told me to keep going, but I don't because if they had said I should play it safe and take a desk job, I wouldn't have listened. I didn't decide to follow a dream—I was kidnapped by it—and if you feel like it's a choice at all, you should choose not to, because the ones who make it were either born with it or felt they'd rather let it kill them rather than die inside from doing anything else."[9]

SAUL: When I asked a very motivated, talented, 16-year-old cyclist what her ultimate goal in cycling was, she replied, "I want to represent the U.S.A. in the Olympics…and win a medal." I answered, "That's a really impressive, challenging goal. If that's what you aspire to, then what do you have to do to make it happen?" We discussed how challenging, meaningful goals drive athletes to do the fitness training for greater power and endurance, the technical work for riding skill and cycling smarts, and the mental strength training to become more focused, confident, and mentally tougher. Next, I asked her, "How old will you be when you compete and excel in the Olympics?" She thought for a moment. "Around 24 or 25." I responded, "That's eight or nine years from now. How would you be different then, from the rider you are now?" She answered, "I'd be stronger, more powerful, smarter...more experienced, more skilled, more positive, and mentally tougher." I smiled. "That's a good response. You seem to be a very intelligent and positive person. The path to performing at the highest level and achieving your goals is working every day on the things you just described."

Encouraging a developing rider to actually imagine what he or she would look and feel like as an Olympian can inspire them to do the necessary work to achieve their goal.

CYCLE WISDOM

"I think the biggest mental quality is just having a single-mindedness. It's almost an obsessive trend I guess. Especially when it comes to sport. Obviously doing any professional sport at the highest level requires the athlete to be so focused on the outcome, the goal of getting to that highest level, that it basically takes over your mind and everything you do from the moment you wake up in the morning until you go to sleep at night is geared towards achieving that goal. I think that as an athlete I definitely fall into that category. And passion drives that single-mindedness."

—Chris Froome, Great Britain, 4x Tour de France Champion[10]

CYCLE WISDOM

"For me the way to strengthen one's mental game is by setting micro goals on the way to a larger attainable goal. I always liked to have a goal. You need a goal that's out there that you are working towards. But setting those attainable goals helps your mind to think, okay, I just got this goal, now I can get to the next one, and the next one. You're programming your mind so you are always getting somewhere."

—Alex Stieda, Canada, First North American to don the Tour de France Yellow Jersey[11]

Intermediate Goals

We recommend setting goals for each season. Define the specifics of what you want to achieve in that time period, set the training and competition plan to make it happen, and then DO THE WORK. It may be helpful to talk with your coach(es) in creating your intermediate goal plans.

PEGGY: Goals for the off-season are the same. Have a realistic picture of what you want to accomplish over that time frame. For some, it's going to be maintaining fitness and not gaining weight. It's the time that cyclists test equipment, positions, clothing, and nutrition. Skills are improved and cross-training is employed to rebalance the body. Strength training is a mainstay in most cyclists' off-season. The off-season is also a good time for some mental training.

Short-Term Goals

Set short-term goals for your next workout and your next event. There is considerable evidence that the best way to grow your ability is with deliberate practice. That is, focused practice that pushes you to improve specific skills, as opposed to practice that just goes over some of the same things you have already developed.

PEGGY: For a training example: An athlete I coach wants to break 24 minutes in a local time trial. We determined that he can really improve his cadence at race effort. His measurable goal then is to race with cadence above 100 rpm for 24 minutes. The short-term goals progress from where he is now–under 90 rpm–up to the 24 minutes, like this:

> 100 rpm for 5 minutes–by middle of March
> 100 rpm for 10 minutes–by end of April
> 100 rpm for 15 minutes–by end of May
> 100 rpm for 20 minutes–by end of June

The gearing, and thus wattage, will vary with the intensity of his training phases, but the progression is clear in that it is measurable, challenging, and motivating. He also has a training partner to match him in this task and keep him accountable. Individual workouts break down the effort into 30-second or minute segments, linked together with recovery time. Within the short-term goals are workouts progressing like this:

1. 2 sets of 30 seconds on, 30 seconds off x5
2. 1 minute on, 1 minute off x5
3. 2 minutes on, 2 minutes off x3
4. 3 minutes on, 3 minutes off x2
5. 5 minutes on, 5 minutes off x1

This short-term progression can be doubled for the next phase, and so on. Progressions like these ensure success by being obtainable and measurable.

Challenging goals and an effective practice plan are essential for developing and improving power, skill, and performance. It's important to work on both strengths and weaknesses. Work on strengths to build and maintain your positive edge on the competition and grow confidence. Work on areas that need improvement, so they are no longer deficiencies. Your goals are for you. Set goals that inspire you.

CYCLE WISDOM

"Cycling's not just about who's the best at exercising, it's also about those skills of descending, and those skills of position. I do a lot of visualization. I write down a lot of goals. I write down where I want to be in position entering into a key feature, how I see the race playing out. I spend a lot of time working on those aspects of the sport."

—Michael Woods, Canada, Winner of the 100th Edition of Milano–Torino, Tour de France Stage Winner, Pro Road World Championships Medalist[12]

Team Goals

Your personal goals as a teammate can add to or detract from team culture and a winning team mindset.

CYCLE WISDOM

"We are interested in a rider's qualities as a teammate, as much as we are in their physical talents or skills. Cycling is very much a team sport, wherein riders are expected to subordinate their personal results to those of the team's goals, including supporting the team's race leader. This also requires a rider to give his absolute best, in the world's toughest sport, and absolutely emptying the tank when required. Such special domestique riders are highly coveted by teams, nearly as much as the stars who win the races."

—Sylvan Adams, Canada/Israel, 2x Masters World Champion, UCI Pro Series Team Israel–Premier Tech Co-Owner[13]

You can discuss your goals with a coach, share them with your team, or you can keep them private. The key is that your goals are clearly defined, there is an activity plan to achieve them, and you do the work every day to make them a reality. This includes running the right positive mental focus while improving the physiological and skill components, and building confidence in all areas. Improvement is made by assessing where you currently are, and what you need to achieve to meet the goal. Statements like, *I want to win the local race* or *I want to beat Sally*, are motivators, but they are not markers of improvement. With measurable goals you can plan, view, and track improvements. You picked up this book to help you improve your cycling. Now, before you set some goals, let's do some self-evaluation.

EXERCISE 2.1

Self-Assessment

It's essential to evaluate where you are now, so you can have a starting point for goal setting. Self-evaluation highlights your strengths and weaknesses. For the greatest benefit, be completely honest with yourself in doing this assessment.

Rate yourself on a scale of 1 to 7 in the following categories.
(1 = very weak/poor, 7 = very strong/excellent)

Cycling Smarts

- Your ability to use your strengths to your best advantage ____
- Your ability to read opponents' strengths and weaknesses ____
- Your ability to use time and space effectively ____
- Your ability to listen to and act on coach's/manager's input ____

Your Motivation

- How hard you are working to achieve your long-term goals ____
- Your commitment to becoming the best cyclist you can be ____
- Your commitment to your fitness training ____
- Your commitment to your skills training ____
- Your commitment to your mental training ____

Your Fitness

- Your cycling endurance ____
- Your fitness compared to your competitors' fitness ____
- Your fitness compared to the top 10 in your world level ____

Your Skill

- Your basic skills (pedaling, cadence, shifting) ____
- You ability to push on flat terrain ____
- Your ability to climb, sitting and standing ____
- Your ability to corner and descend ____
- Your ability at starts and sprints ____

Emotional Management

- Your confidence level ____
- Your ability to be calm under pressure ____
- Your ability to act on coach's/manager's instruction ____
- Your ability to stay focused and in control when something negative happens (e.g., a flat tire, a mechanical, missing a break or directive/instructions) ____
- Your general ability to get along with others ____

Mental Toughness

- You are a fighter who loves to compete ____
- Nothing takes you off task ____

U.S. Masters criterium champion, Mark Light, conducted a similar self-assessment regarding his criterium efficiency strategy.

> "I realized that the average criterium pace was 27 mph, and the classic pedaling efficiency standard of 90 rpm meant that the 53 x 14 was the most efficient race gear. So I worked on smooth pedaling in that gear, five minutes at a time, a few times per ride, a few rides per week. No junk miles, no group rides, no tempo…just that. After a few weeks, I really knew

> how to ride that gear super efficiently. I knew I had a heritage of athletic success in my family, but doing a self-assessment was key. You have to know your realm."[14]

PEGGY: Everything he did, from cornering around alleyways to doing interval training behind accelerating tractor trailers, contributed to his ensuing win.

HOMEWORK

There are two steps in using this book. First, read and understand the material. Second, do the work. You know if you go to the gym and lift weights, you will get stronger. However, knowing that and not going to the gym or doing the work, changes nothing. To get the most out of the book and the Cycle Psyched program, we strongly encourage you to work with the exercises and the homework.

Goal Setting

1. What is your ultimate long-term (dream) goal? Use the self-assessment above to compare where you are now, to where you want to be in your ultimate goal. Determine what it will take to achieve this goal.
2. What are some (seasonal) intermediate goals to get there?
3. What are some short-term goals (e.g., workouts, upcoming competitions)?

Continue to evaluate yourself as you progress (or have setbacks) and adjust your goals accordingly.

CHAPTER 3
Power Thinking

CYCLE WISDOM

"Your thoughts shape your reality. Think power thoughts like *smooth and fast*, *I can*, and *I corner well*. You get more of what you think about. Positive thought creates positive results. Use power words and affirmations."

—*Peggy and Saul*[15]

Technical Thoughts

Specific thoughts that relate to your technique on the bicycle.

PEGGY: Good habits like being down in the drops of road handlebars while cornering or descending might require self-reminders like *down, elbows bent, exhale*, or *lean the bike, not your body*, or *look where you want to go*. These are thoughts we use in workouts and training to develop excellent racing habits.

CYCLE WISDOM

"When I first came into cycling, I just assumed that because I was one of the better runners for my age in the world that I'd transition into cycling easily. However, that's not the case. Cycling is such a skill-oriented sport. There are guys in this world that are stronger than me but that don't come close to beating me because at this point, my race IQ, my race skills, are far higher. But it took a long time to get there. I spent a lot of time strategizing and working on ways of improving my skills.... It's been an evolution, something I really respect as a part of the sport."

—Michael Woods, Canada, Winner of the 100th Edition of Milano–Torino, Tour de France Stage Winner, Pro Road Race World Championships Medalist[16]

Strategy Thoughts

Thoughts prior to a competition that essentially give us a flexible blueprint to performing in the competition.

PEGGY: One of my pet peeves is when racers say their race strategy is to *see how it goes*. The assessing part is good, but it leaves out what to do in any scenarios. A better general race strategy is to be positive about your position and effort. You could say *I am going to stay with the top five riders, I pounce like a cat*, or *I'm calm under pressure and I cover the moves*.

Michael Woods

CYCLE WISDOM

"Races aren't only run like a marathon. You have to have the pain tolerance of a marathon runner, but then, you have to be lucid enough...because this isn't a sport of just pushing yourself. This is also a chess game on wheels. You have to be reading the race—should I save my energy for the next hill? Is this the hill? You have to be constantly thinking. And you have to absolutely be willing to risk everything."

—Johathan Vaughters, U.S.A., Former Pro Racer, UCI WorldTeam EF Education–Easy Post Manager[17]

Personal Thoughts

Thoughts that describe the way a cyclist thinks about him or herself. They reflect self-image and a general sense of confidence.

SAUL: Early in the mental coaching process I encourage cyclists to actively think of themselves in a positive way.

- Every morning when you wake up, look at yourself in the mirror, say to yourself *I am a good cyclist.* Or if that is a work in progress, say *I am becoming a good cyclist.*
- Then list five or six strengths you have as a rider. Typical responses include:
  - *I am smart. I have a good racing sense.*
  - *I am skilled. I handle the bike well in corners, sprints, on climbs and descents.*
  - *I have great form, good body position, a fluid pedal stroke.*
  - *I am strong, powerful (on climbs, on the flats, in sprints, in technical sections)*
  - *I am fit.*
  - *I am mentally tough, committed, and determined.*

Power Words

Power words can be used to build and strengthen confidence and a positive mindset. When we spoke about managing your mental computer, we stated, "You are the boss." As such, you are in control. You are response-able to control and create power thoughts and feelings in any situation.

Attack and *smooth* are two power words that Saul has used in every sport, and they certainly apply in cycling. Attack and smooth are the yin and yang of riding and racing. Either you are putting the pedal to the metal and pushing to go as fast as you can—*attack*. Or you are smoothing it out, giving yourself more flow, which is pacing and balancing and will ultimately lead to more efficiency and speed—*smooth*.

PEGGY: In events such as downhill mountain bike racing or BMX, *attack* and *smooth* are extremely useful because the whole race is about attacking and then instantly shifting gears to smoothing, finessing, controlling, and handling the bike well through rough spots, rocks, and down steep drops and turns in the course. The result is a smooth flow, guiding the bike over and around the course. Then, as the course flattens out again, it becomes attack, attack, attack, turn the wheel, accelerate, hammer, pump, push, go. Success is directly related to your ability to anticipate the shift from attacking to going smoothly, and to reacting well at the right time. It's similar on the road. There are times when you are pacing, smoothing and working on good flow and an efficient use of energy. Then, as you move to an incline or into a sprint situation, you think *attack* and become aggressive. With training, the power word *attack* can create a feeling that will spark you to spin the breathing wheel deeper and push for power. The word *smooth* can remind you to smooth out that flow of energy through your body. And smooth can also mean speed.

CYCLE WISDOM

"I've worked on my down-hilling, and I've gotten a lot smoother. Go smooth and you go fast."

—Tinker Juarez, U.S.A., Pro BMX Grand National Champion, 4x NORBA Cross-Country, 4x 24-Hour Solo National Champion[18]

Here are two types of cues for *attack*.

1. The first is dictated by the terrain of the course. Difficult terrain such as climbs, open windy roads, technical trails, and tight turns, require more physical effort and skill. The successful rider pours effort into these challenges and avoids wasting energy in futile efforts like attacking on straight descents where others can easily follow or little time can be gained.
2. The second is determined by strategic action in the race, such as final lap, prime laps, or counter-attacking someone else's aggressive move. The successful rider conserves energy by smoothing between efforts and puts more energy into well-timed attacks.

For example:

Instead of:	**Do this:**
Riding out in the wind	Draft others' wheels to move up
Initiating numerous attacks	Wait and put more into one, well-timed attack
Attacking on a downhill	Attack out of a corner or at the top of a climb
Pulling at the front	Attack from the top third of the group

And the list goes on. The more you practice reading the terrain and the action of the race, the better you can get at predicting the final outcome. The goal is to recognize winning moves and to take the opportunities to make these moves.

CYCLE WISDOM

"In prepping for the New Jersey state road championships, I decided that if I was still in the lead break on the final lap, I would attack at a specific spot...where there was a colorful mailbox on the side of the road. Having rehearsed that, saying 'at this mailbox I will attack,' when I hit that spot I attacked automatically and was able to take the win as if on autopilot."

—David Kahl, U.S.A., New Jersey State Masters Road Champion[19]

By using visualization, you can experience races in your head and practice your response to the attack and smooth cues. The faster your actual response time, the bigger advantage you have over your opponents. Athletes who think too much or listen to negative inner dialogue (*I'm tired, I'm not sure I can do this*) often miss the moment.

CYCLE WISDOM

"The main thing is blocking out those demons that are telling you to ease up. You think you are tired but suddenly you just find new limits."

—Geraint Thomas, Great Britain, 2x Olympic Gold Medalist, Tour de France Winner[20]

Race Talk

SAUL: I asked riders: "Do you ever talk to yourself, say things to yourself to keep you focused while you are racing?"

CHRIS FROOME: It sounds a bit ridiculous, but the biggest thing I do is count. I find it distracts me from any negative thoughts, and it keeps my mind busy. I think as athletes we are prone to doubting ourselves or looking for an escape. I mean your body is hurting, you want to slow down, you want to give up, and you're almost thinking of justifications in your mind as to why you can; this didn't go right today, so it's okay if I come second or third today, or whatever. And I find if I count, stupid things like kilometer markers to the finish, it helps. If I count the last 10 kilometers to the finish, just literally down, I know in a few 100 meters I'll be at nine and then at nine, I'll be at eight, and then I'm just three away from five, and five is halfway. I break it down into manageable chunks. And I'll literally be having these conversations in my head while I'm racing. I'll be working out how much further to the next kilometer marker, and then how much further that is to the finish. A lot of the time, I will have worked out beforehand how long it would take to do the climb. Let's say it's going to take 18 minutes, I'll also do the same, either with kilometer markers or with the time, just counting down, like, okay, I know I'm under 10 minutes to go now, and literally counting each minute as it goes past, that keeps my mind busy, and it keeps me away from any negative thoughts about giving up or slowing down.[21]

GUY SURGIV: It depends on the race. If I'm really in the zone, or heading towards the finish line. One of my career highlights was when I won the Israeli Nationals for the first time. It was a sprint, and I won on the finish line by a half wheel. And I was far behind...but I never gave up 'til I crossed the finish line, and that's how I won. Since then, I have this sentence in my mind going for me.

It's never over until it's over. It keeps me going even in very tough moments, even when it looks like the race is over. You never give up until you cross the finish line. That's the best you can do.[22]

Reel 'em in: When you see riders ahead of you, the thought *reel 'em in* is another power phrase and image that can give some direction to your energy. Reeling them in is about intention. The word intention comes from a root word that means *sending out the mind. Reel 'em in* can express the feeling and image of sending out your mind and hooking the other riders, drawing them to you/or you to them and closing the gap.

PEGGY: Some riders extend this concept, using a fishing rod image to reel in their minute man in a time trial or a break that's up the road. They visually hook their sights on the other rider and use their cranks as the fishing reel, spinning faster to reel them in. Interestingly, the component manufacturer Shimano, is also known for their fishing reels.

Other riders think about being chased and are motivated by the fear of being overtaken. We believe it is always better to project yourself forward. Keep your focus ahead to a point at which you can project your power and ride aggressively, rather than looking over your shoulder and riding out of fear, which produces tension. Many races have been famously lost by a competitor looking back for an opponent, only to get nipped at the line.

SAUL: I was with the Canadian cycling team at the Tour of Texas, a spring race series. We were using the Tour to get ready for the Olympic Games. There were road races all around Texas. The one that I want to talk about was a road race that took place near Austin, Texas. When you work with fifteen or twenty cyclists in a camp, there are always some who are more interested and responsive to what you are presenting…and some who are not. Marie-Claude Audet was a talented, young, road racer who expressed a strong interest in the sport psychology aspect of racing. We had spent some training time together, and she seemed to find it helpful. I was hoping she would do well in the Austin road race. I was standing at the side of the road watching the race, when true to form, a small group of five lead riders (the breakaway group), whizzed by. About twenty seconds later, they were followed by a solitary rider, Audet, and then, about thirty seconds after that, by a large group comprising the rest of the field. After they all passed, I wondered what happened with Audet. Would she make it up to the breakaway group or be sucked back into the pack?

A couple of hours later, Audet finished the race:

> "I was so angry when I missed the break that I just made up my mind that I was going to get them. So I just focused on sending my energy out to them and reeling them in. As I was chasing, I got way ahead of the pack…and I was gaining on the breakaway group. That's probably when you saw me. But before I could get there, I started to wonder where the rest of the pack was. And that was the strange part because as I thought of the group behind me…I seemed to lose energy and direction…and slowly I got drawn back into the pack."[23]

As previously noted, the word intention comes from a root word meaning *to stretch out*. There is no more illustrative example of stretching out the mind, than the intention of trying to catch up to the breakaway group in a road race. When Audet's intention was focused on the breakaway group, it was a possibility. When her focus shifted to those behind her, the mind stretch disappeared, and so did the possibility of catching the leaders.

CYCLE WISDOM

"People regularly talk themselves out of superior race performances by holding onto positions they are comfortable with. You have to not be afraid to take risk. You've got to be prepared to engage in tactics that could make you lose the race if you don't win, but rather that than settling for that 12th place that you know you can get anytime. Cyclists can also hold themselves back by thinking too far ahead. They think they are in the right break, but the pace is too high, it's too far to go to the finish and they can't hold on, and they drift back to the pack. Instead, if they break it down to one mile or kilometer at a time, the task at hand, they can make it."

—Larry Towner, U.S.A., New Jersey State Champion, Coach at ProPower Coaching[24]

Staying totally focused on the task at hand, Jennifer Valente won an Olympic gold medal in the omnium event in Tokyo.

> "Before the Points Race I was leading [in overall omnium points], but it was pretty close. So I really just approached it like any other single race. Taking it one event at a time and one sprint at a time, and looking at it as an individual race and trying to put the idea of an Olympic medal on the back burner for the moment I just focused on the race that was about to begin."[25]

PEGGY: I was taught to never look across the track at my challenger in the pursuit event. Looking takes your focus off your task at hand and allows your mind to wander to thoughts about who will win. Keep focused on what tasks you need to attend to, until you are over the finish line.

When you decide to go for it, then go for it!

CYCLE WISDOM

"When you make a move, even if you realize it's the wrong move, go with it. I've lost races because I started a move and stopped. That's one of the things I've carried through my career."

—Connie Paraskevin, U.S.A., 4x World Sprint Champion, Olympic Medalist[26]

Power words and race self-talk should be strong enough that they create a feeling and a picture that increase your power, direction, and potential. There are many types of power words you can use. Be creative. Make the race more of a game. Be in the moment. Be a hunter. Be a cat ready to pounce.

EXERCISE 3.1

Select Power Words

Incorporate a few power words into your cycling. Select words that appeal to you and that are clear and strong enough to give you a positive image or feeling. For them to have any potency or juice in an intense race situation, you have to repeatedly train these words into your mind in practice.

One suggestion is to define and select a few key words before you go out to ride. Consciously and repeatedly use these words at appropriate times as you train until they become part of your cycling self-talk. In our experience, the most helpful power words in bicycle racing are *attack* and *smooth*.

Fear, Pain, and Difficulty

The use of power words is extremely helpful in dealing with the intense pressure and pain that are often part of competitive racing. Here is an example of how Saul used power words to help a cycling team prepare for the Olympics, which resulted in them riding an incredible race.

SAUL: I was asked to work with Canada's team time trial (TTT) in preparation for the Olympic Games. The team had to make a specific qualifying time of 2 hours, 5 minutes, and 10 seconds for the 100 km race in order to qualify for the Olympics. The challenge was their personal best time was 2 hours, 6 minutes, and 40 seconds. In other words, they had to take 1 minute and 30 seconds off their best time ever just to qualify. I began with some relaxation and conscious breathing training. Then I asked the four riders what specific thoughts and feelings came to mind in racing that could cause them to tighten up and lose power. They identified three biggies: fear, pain, and difficulty.

Fear

Racers fear losing control, breaking down, failure, embarrassment, crashing, getting injured, and letting the team down. For most, fear is a high-frequency performance thought. It's one that can stimulate action or cause tension, contraction, limited breathing, and reduced power.

CYLCE WISDOM

"Fear is something you have to learn to control and use to your advantage because everyone has it. The difference is how you let if affect you. You have to be confident."

—Missy "Missile" Giove, U.S.A., Downhill Mountain Bike World Champion[27]

Pain

The pain most frequently experienced in cycling is a physical pain so intense at times that a rider can't continue to race. Some even pass out on their bicycles. Then there is the psychic pain that both racers and non-racers experience in relation to the possibility of a failed performance. Psychic pain threatens the ego. Like physical pain, it can also cause contraction, limit breathing, and cut down power.

Difficulty

Difficulty under race circumstances, involve thoughts and feelings like *this is too hard*, *it's impossible*, *there's no way*, and *I can't do this*. These also cause contraction, limit breathing, and cut down power.

SAUL: I asked each TTT rider to come up with a single power thought they could tune into whenever they experienced fear, pain, or difficulty. The thought was to be simple, brief, and powerful, a single word that was personally meaningful and that stimulated positive feelings. The stress and fatigue of a race can express themselves like static or snow on sound waves, making it difficult to focus or think straight. We wanted a power word that would be comprehensible and useful under pressure.

Each rider selected a different word. Brian, the team captain, chose the word *more*. Whenever he experienced pain, fatigue, self-doubt, or negativity, he would think *more*, turn the wheel, and push a little harder, a little longer, a little faster, a little *more*. Yvon chose the word *smooth*. He was a big guy who knew that under pressure, he tended to tighten up which caused him to have to work harder to accomplish the same result. Chris chose the word *machine*. He wanted to experience himself as inhuman and impervious to pain, doubt, and difficulty. Whenever he noticed himself tuning into a limiting thought or feeling, Chris would take a breath, draw in energy, turn the wheel, think *machine*, and accelerate. Dave chose the word *fast*. It sparked in him the image of being lighter, more aggressive, and streamlined. He brought that power word to mind whenever he felt stressed.

Part of this psychological training addressed dealing effectively with the considerable fear, pain, and difficulty produced by that punishing, 100 km event. I explained to each rider that the natural reaction to these three main thoughts and feelings is to contract, tighten up, and try to hold on. It is much easier to be aggressive than it is to hold on. Holding on doesn't change anything. It just means that you attempt to ride the race in the state of being tense and contracted. And it is way more difficult to be fast and to endure in that contracted, limited state. Along with thought management, the riders also worked on conscious breathing and release techniques, so if/when they felt fear, pain, or difficulty, they could focus on their breathing, tuning into their positive power word, and turning the wheel.

In the race to qualify for the Olympics, the team went out very fast. After 20 km, Chris reported that he started to feel pain and was thinking, *I hurt, I won't be able to keep this pace*. Then he thought, *hold on*. When he realized what he was thinking, he reminded himself, *it's easier to be aggressive than to hold on*. So he went deeper into his breathing, refocused on his power word *machine*, and picked up his pace. Again, about 70 km into the race, Chris focused on and locked into pain. Again, the negative thoughts followed, *I can't continue*. Again, he caught himself and refocused on his breathing and on being like a *machine*. He rode right through the pain. He rode a great race. The whole team did.

What makes this story still relevant is the bottom line. The riders went out at a fast pace and stayed focused and aggressive throughout the race. Dave, Chris, and Yvon all mentioned to me afterward that when they were hurting, they entertained the thoughts of, *I can't do it, I can't keep the pace, I can't go on*. When they noticed themselves tuning into those negative thoughts and feelings, they remembered to go deeper into their breathing, to turn the wheel, to generate more power, and to refocus on their power word.

They rode the 100 km distance in 1:51:10. Their time was a remarkable 15 and a half minutes faster than the previous Canadian record, and an unofficial world record in that event. What is also impressive is that it wasn't a new team of superstars imported from another part of the planet or the galaxy. Three of the four racers had been part of the team that set the 2:06:40 TTT record the year before. The difference now was that all the key elements were in place. The right people were selected, they were well coached, they knew what to do, and they were in excellent shape. And they were trained to manage their minds aggressively, to change limiting thoughts and feelings, and to stay tuned into winning by using their power words.

An amusing side story to this account of power words leading to excellence involves one of the alternate team racers from the four-man, back-up team. This particular racer had a history of not performing well whenever he rode for the national team. When he raced for his club, he was daring and aggressive. But as soon as he put on that national team jersey, he became tentative and defensive. Instead of *going for it,* his focus became, *don't make a mistake, don't let the team down*. Instead of projecting his mind forward and out along the course, and *reeling 'em in*, he focused on his feet and counting his pedal strokes to make sure he didn't pull less than his share. The dominant thought patterns he ran were, *don't let them down, they're watching*, and *they're counting on you*. His focus was the ubiquitous *them* and what others were thinking about him and his performance. Consequently, the power word we selected for him to focus on was *f– 'em*. Whenever he felt himself tightening up and thinking a negative thought, he would take a breath, draw in power, think *f– 'em*, and turn the wheel.

I had asked each of the riders to write out their power word and stick it onto the back of the seat of the bicycle in front of them, so as they rode on that wheel, they would have a visual reminder of their power word. The Olympic qualification race was held on a blocked-off section of the Trans-Canada Highway outside of Vancouver, B.C. Prior to the start, a crowd of cycling enthusiasts, friends, and supporters milled around examining the state-of-the-art bicycles. With curiosity they read the words on the back of each seat, *more, smooth, machine, fast*, and then the back up team rider's *f– em*. On seeing this last word, some spectators did a double-take, others glared at the obscenity. The rider inevitably flushed. "It's not my word." But, of course, no one had any idea what he was talking about.

Affirmations

Affirmations or power thoughts are simply positive statements about who you are, what you want to create, and what you are in the process of manifesting. They can relate to skill, conditioning, strategy, and attitude. For example: *I am an excellent sprinter, I deserve to be in the breakaway, I focus well in time trials, I am good at technical mountain biking, I ride smoothly and steadily*. Repetition builds strength. By repeating these thoughts to yourself you can grow a more positive mindset. One that can nurture optimal effort and a greater sense of well-being.

We encourage athletes to combine thoughts and feelings. Take a breath and repeat your power thoughts. Saul frequently makes recordings for athletes combining relaxation and breathing with their power thoughts. The process involved in selecting these thoughts begins with exploring how you want to feel, defining what you want to achieve, and then creating an affirmation or power thought that you feel comfortable and positive about saying to yourself.

EXERCISE 3.2

Select Affirmations

Review the affirmations listed below. Determine which ones might work well for you. Select those that relate to your situation, that address your strengths or aspects of cycling that you want to develop, or those that just feel good.

Select or create 8–10 affirmations or power thoughts that would help you become a more powerful, positive rider. Write them down and repeat them to yourself often. You can say your affirmations to yourself or write them in the first person. The first person is personal and powerful, *I am smooth. I am a power machine.* Or you can affirm in the second person. In our day-to-day lives, people usually address us in the second person. It's both effective and pleasant to hear positive things about us in the second person, *You are a star. You use everything.*

Cycling Affirmations

Here are some thoughts to repeat to yourself. Select those that feel good to you and highlight what you want to create or feel. After each thought, take a breath. Remember, thoughts precede action, and repetition builds strength. This list of affirmations was used by the Canadian Cycling Team at a pre-Olympic training camp.

- I am the boss. I control my mind.
- I have a personal connection to unlimited energy and power.
- I am a power channel. Energy flows through me like a star.
- I am electric.
- I am jet powered.
- I am quick and strong as a cat.
- I use my speed and timing perfectly.
- I am a big cheetah (or panther).
- I am a power machine. I am smoothness and power.
- My breath is a power pump.
- Some free breathing and a little adrenaline are like jet fuel.
- I am consistent and tireless like ocean waves.
- I can depend on my legs for speed and power.
- I pedal big gears with speed and smoothness.
- I am one with my bike.
- I am mentally tough.
- My mind is a force I use to make things happen.
- I use everything for more power.
- I use pain as positive feedback.
- I use it all to make me tougher, faster, and hungrier to win.
- I deserve to express 100% of my ability.
- There is nothing to prevent me from giving 100%.
- I ride like the wind. I use the wind.
- I cut through the wind like a knife.
- I find something positive in every situation.
- I use the tough days, the hills, and the class riders to push myself to be tougher, stronger, and faster.
- I take strength from drafting others.
- I get strength from challenging and catching others.
- I have everything I need to be a gold medal racer.

- I recall the feelings I've had on great days.
- I tune out irrelevant thoughts and worries.
- I enjoy winning.
- Self-love is allowing myself to win.
- I deserve to feel good. Feeling good and recharging are an important part of my total preparation.
- I am a winner.

Speed Affirmations

A time trial racer at the World Championships was given the following list of personal affirmations by Saul, along with the instructions to read each thought, take a breath, and let it sink in. Remember, repetitions build strength. Afterward, the racer set a flying 200-meter world record.

- I am a power machine.
- I am tapped into an unlimited supply of power.
- I have power pads, a cat's feet.
- My legs are pistons.
- With each breath, I draw in power.
- I send power out in front of me, and down my legs and feet.
- I cut through air like a knife.
- I am ease and power.
- The more I ride, the faster I go.
- I am light and strong, like a big cat.
- I ride faster and faster.
- Pain is power.
- I use everything.
- Nothing distracts me.
- My focus is energy in, energy out, ease and power, faster and faster.
- I deserve to express all of my ability, to be as great as I can be.

SAUL: Words are like food for the spirit. They can nurture us. Just as you wouldn't eat food that you don't like, it's important that you say things to yourself that feel good to you and give you power. Repetition builds strength. Repeating power words, phrases, and thoughts builds mental strength. Repeat them frequently. Develop a positive mental focus and attitude. In relaxing and challenging situations, take a breath and affirm the positive.

PEGGY: Remember to use breathing when you are repeating affirmations or imaging with power thoughts. The positive feeling should come first. If you match the positive feeling with the positive thought, you create a loop that feeds itself with positive energy.

HOMEWORK

Smooth & Attack Affirmations

1. Review several past races or rides in terms of smooth and attack. Label each part of the course *smooth* or *attack*. Do the same for your overall strategy of the event, noting where to smooth and where to attack with your energy.
2. Select eight to ten affirmations. Repeat them daily—in the morning, before riding, and during riding. Some people tape a list of their favorite affirmations to the mirror and look at themselves while repeating them. Observe what works for you.

We have begun the process of Right Focus. Use power words and thoughts to replace negative or anxiety-charged thoughts that might come to mind. Work at shifting your thinking with positive thoughts and affirmations to overcome fear, pain, and difficulty, and you will develop a powerful performance tool.

CHAPTER 4
High-Performance Imagery

The goal of this chapter is to explore three different ways to use imagery to enhance your cycling performance and enjoyment of the sport. Images are primal. We experience images even before we use words. Imagery can be a powerful component of our ability to focus. If a picture is worth a thousand words, dynamic imagery can be a training manual. If we want the Right Focus, we want to choose powerful, high-performance images.

There are three basic kinds of images.

1. Goal Imagery
2. Stimulating Imagery
3. Mental Rehearsal

Goal Imagery

Imagine a successful end result.

Create and hold the image of exactly what it is you are working toward. That can be both your ultimate goal in cycling (e.g., competing successfully in the Olympics or World Championship), or it can be the end result of an upcoming race event. As seen in Chapter 2, a clear and meaningful goal is a driver. It pushes you to do the physical, tactical, and mental preparation to make that result a reality.

Most sport psychologists would say that it is more important to think about the process of getting there rather than simply focusing on the end result. We agree. However, visualizing yourself on the winner's podium, seeing yourself smiling after successfully completing a century ride, seeing yourself crossing the finish line with your arms in the air, taking photos at the top of an arduous climb, all are inspiring images that may help you sustain the drive to realize your goals. Of course, the successful image is no substitute for the effort and hard work required. But imagining the successful end result can certainly be empowering. Albert Einstein summed up the importance of imagery in leading to successful end results with, "Imagination is everything. It is the preview of life's coming attractions."[28]

EXERCISE 4.1

Goal Imagery

Imagine your successful end result. See yourself crossing the finish line. Are you pumping your fist in the air? Are you on the podium, having a medal placed around your neck? Are you seeing a world record time on the scoreboard? How will you celebrate your achievement?

Stimulating Imagery

Become a hunter.

SAUL: To help athletes in many sports excel, I have recommended they use stimulating images which inspire and spur them on to greater effort and achievement. I begin by asking cyclists this question: If you were to pick an animal that would give you qualities you would want to have in order to race your best, what animal would you choose? The animals that most riders select have been the big cats: cheetahs, leopards, jaguars, cougars, panthers, and tigers. Some have picked eagles and wolves. The idea is that as human beings each of us has qualities that are angelic and animalistic. The angelic part of us is that aspect that has the capacity to envision things, and then manifest them. We set a goal, we envision it, we work/train to make it happen and then, sometimes, remarkably, it manifests. Our angelic aspect can use thought and imagery to shape our destiny. We create and hold pictures of the future that can become our ultimate reality. Our animal aspect can bring instinctive awareness and power. We can use imagery to awaken the animal spirit that is within us, allowing us to become hunters.

CYCLE WISDOM

"You can't mountain bike and think about dinner or divorce or the bills. You need to be one big sensory receptor if you are going to stay within the margins of control. You need to be like an animal. They don't think about bills."

—Jacquie Phelan, U.S.A., NORBA Mountain Bike XC Champion[29]

SAUL: When I ask elite athletes to select an animal image, 99% choose predators. Predators are hunters. Cyclists most commonly choose the big cats and wolves. These animals have tremendous power, balance, and speed. They are assertive. They are hunters. They are crafty and smart. And unlike some cyclists, if the prey eludes them, there is no negative self-judgement; they simply seek out the next prey. They keep hunting. By selecting a cheetah or tiger, you can identify with a power source that has courage and heart, supra-human quickness and speed, as well as remarkable strength, balance, and reflexes conducive to effective attacks and hunts. Animal images can provide great power. The animal you choose should represent you at your best. When you say to yourself the word *cheetah*, *tiger*, *jaguar*, or whatever your image is, allow it to awaken the animal in you, to stimulate you to spin the wheel. Spinning the wheel fires up the cheetah. It intensifies your speed, jump, and power.

CYCLE WISDOM

"If you are going to race, you've got to have the heart of a lion. That's what makes one racer different from another, what distinguishes a winner from all the others."

—Joe Tosi, U.S.A., Racer, Coach (Tosi's quote coined the phrase "Hearts of Lions," used by author Peter Nye to title his book Hearts of Lions *about the history of cycling in the U.S.A.)*[30]

CYCLE WISDOM

"I imagine I'm a cat ready to land anywhere."

—Paul Willerton, U.S.A., Road and Mountain Bike Pro[31]

CYCLE WISDOM

"I imagine I am an eagle soaring, watching, ready to attack."

—Peggy Maass Labiuk, U.S.A., 2x National Champion, World Championships Medalist, Ultra Marathon World Record Holder[32]

SAUL: I was doing an evening seminar on sport psychology and cycling for a group of cyclists and triathletes. They were a mix of competitive and recreational athletes. We had talked about conscious breathing for power and ease, about emotional control, power thoughts, affirmations, and imagery. One woman asked a question about something many riders have experienced. "When I'm descending fast, the thought sometimes pops into my mind that I am going too fast and that I could crash. When that happens, I notice that I tense up and slow right down. I just can't seem to get that fearful, negative thought out of my mind. Is there something you can recommend that I could do?" Earlier, I had asked this woman what animal image she would choose to enhance her cycling performance. She had said, "A dog." When I queried what kind of dog she was imaging, she replied, "My cocker spaniel. I really enjoy running and cycling with my cocker spaniel." I made note of her remark at the time without commenting on it. But now that she was asking for advice about descending with speed, I said, "You appear to be an intelligent and sensitive woman, and you have an active mind. These anxious thoughts you are having are simply your mind trying to protect you. What I suggest is that whenever you experience fear or anxiety, go back to your breathing, release any tension you may be experiencing, and then say something calming and integrating to yourself. An excellent word is *smooth*. And, if you really want to descend with speed, I recommend you change your animal image from a cocker spaniel to a descent specialist like a mountain lion or a cheetah, an animal with incredible agility and balance. What you have done in choosing your pet cocker spaniel is to select something that is comfortable. And, while a part of you may want to descend with speed, it's clear that there's another part of you that wants to feel safe and comfortable. I can't tell you what your intention should be. However, if you want to descend with speed, the cocker spaniel image has got to go." This story describes an anxiety that many athletes (including cyclists) have about losing control, and the conflict between our desire to compete and stretch the boundaries, and our need for comfort and security. It illustrates how any challenging activity (like cycling) can be a mirror that reflects unresolved uncertainties and imbalances.

CYCLE WISDOM

"Hans Rey doesn't ride like a nervous bunny on a pogo stick.... He rides like a leopard: smooth and aggressive."

—*John Olsen, U.S.A., Frame Designer, Trials World Champion, U.S. Mountain Bike Hall of Fame*[33]

Here are examples of animal images used by successful cyclists.

Brian Walton—the wolf
This Olympic silver medalist used the wolf for its ability to hunt both solo or with the pack. He even had a wolf tattooed onto his leg.

Steve Bauer—the tiger
He wore the yellow jersey and won stages of the Tour de France awakening the tiger to remind him to use his breathing, spin the wheel, and fire up.

Felicity Wardlaw—the panther
She used panther imagery to win the Australian national road race title, racing through the panther's eyes.

Bernard Hinault—the badger

The legendary French racer was called the badger for his aggressive nature.

Nelson Vails—the cheetah

He was a sprint phenom, an Olympic and world silver medalist, and Pan American gold medalist. "When I stood on the pedals like the cheetah, I went 100%."[34]

Nelson Vails and his cheetah-painted Canyon bike.

Select the image of an animal that appeals to you. Think about turning the wheel, generating power, and firing up the tiger, panther, cheetah, eagle, or wolf. Be a hunter, power, focused, and fast.

Sport teams often use animal imagery to stimulate competitiveness and support a winning group culture. For example, there are professional sport teams calling themselves lions, tigers, panthers, jaguars, bears, and eagles. Professional cycling is a team sport, and a great example of using animal imagery for building a competitive team culture is the UCI WorldTeam Soudal Quick–Step who call themselves the Wolfpack. It has become a major part of the team's identity and branding. Soudal Quick–Step's CEO Patrick Lefevere said, "We call ourselves 'the Wolfpack.' It's us. The wolf doesn't ever hunt alone. We hunt in a group to victory."[35] Former directeur sportif Brian Holm declared, "It's quite a strong image, isn't it? You don't laugh when the wolfpack is coming. It's a good name. One doesn't want to be known as the white ponies, do you?"[36] Indeed, the hunter wouldn't be a nervous bunny, a white pony, or a pet cocker spaniel.

Team Soudal Quick–Step (the Wolfpack) leading the peloton.

PEGGY: My use of other forms of stimulating imagery helped me to set a world record, riding 490.5 miles in 24 hours, human paced. Before setting the record in Florida, I worked with a massage therapist named Tom Hood. He knew I had strong mental skills and encouraged me to use them while he worked on my body, releasing overworked muscles. One image I liked was of the old pros wearing red felt, medicated patches or plasters to keep their knees warm since they were tough and never wore tights or knee warmers. When my knees ached during the record-setting ride, I imagined I had the red felt on them, warming, relaxing, protecting. At a mandatory rest break, Hood checked me over, quickly pressing his hands over my body. He felt my knees. "You've been working on your knees, haven't you?" He could actually feel a temperature difference in them. My knees were warmer from imagining the red felt on them, and they didn't bother me anymore.

SAUL: At my interdisciplinary pain clinic, one of the most helpful tools to deal with pain was imagery. Imagining warm hands, for example, helped many people reduce the discomfort of headaches. Peggy's example illustrates how one can use creative imagery to reduce pain and increase performance.

Mental Rehearsal

Before an event, actually practice in your mind the things you want to do in competition or on a challenging ride. There are several ways to practice mental rehearsal.

SAUL: A quick and simple approach that I frequently use is to ask riders to visualize six dynamic action images of them doing what they do when they are riding at their best. These could be start images, attack images, riding with power and really cranking it, being streamlined with great body position and aerodynamics, descending smooth and fast, riding confidently in a tight cluster, sprinting, and then pulling away. Bringing to mind and rehearsing these action images before a race or a ride can be empowering and give you the focus and feel of you at your best.

Here is one World Champion cyclist's response to the question, "What are you doing when you are riding at your best?"

- I have a smile on my face.
- My head is on a swivel, fully observing my surroundings.
- I am consistently near the front.
- I am moving through the pack at will, taking the wheels I want.
- I am responding to moves with no hesitation.
- My head is slightly turned to watch the lap board every lap, and I am adjusting my position accordingly.

SAUL: A more in-depth approach to mental rehearsal is to imagine yourself riding a course you have ridden before, and riding it well. First, relax. Take a couple of breaths. Feel energy flowing to you and through you. Relaxing and breathing improve the quality and clarity of your imagery. Now, see yourself on a challenging ride. Imagine feeling good and handling the bike well. You feel strong and smooth. Relax, breathe, experience those feelings. Warm up your mental rehearsal by beginning your imagery with the easy parts. Then gradually imagine you are going through some of the more difficult, challenging parts of the course or competition. See and feel yourself handling these parts well, feeling smooth and powerful. Imagine yourself riding with good technique, using good strategy, and making all the right decisions. There are many reasons why Chris Froome is a 4x Tour de France winner, including his dedication, his thorough preparation, and his impressive use of mental rehearsal. I asked him what he does to prepare mentally for a race.

CHRIS FROOME: For me, this is something very personal. I find visualization helps a lot. I am meticulous about planning as well. It really helps me. I'll just give an example: If I know that on stage 10 of the Tour de France we go up this big mountain, and that's going to be one of the crucial moments of the race, I have to get there and see it beforehand...see the road, see the bends in the road, so I can picture it in my mind. And quite often when I go and do those reconnaissance rides, I'll be able to pick a point on that road where, I'll say, "Right, this is where I am going to make my move...and this is what's going to happen behind me when I make the move. This guy is going to react like that, that guy is going to react like that, this one won't want to chase me because he's going to expect someone else to do it, so this is the moment to attack." And for weeks before I actually get to that point in the road, that stage in the race, I'll be replaying this video in my mind, how I want to see things pan out. And, of course, sport is so unpredictable, I could get to that point in the race, and I could have a flat tire and I wouldn't be able to execute what I was planning, so there are so many things outside of our control. But sometimes my best performances have come on those days when literally I've got to that point in the road, and I've worked myself up so much for that moment where I was going to make the move, or do something that would make a difference in the race, that when I get there, it almost feels as if I'm on autopilot. It doesn't even hurt. The legs don't even hurt even though I'm doing a big effort...or anything.

SAUL: If you are doing this in the Tour, Giro, or one of these stage races, you couldn't have done it the day before that stage, you must have done this well in advance?

CHRIS FROOME: Yeah, generally we would go up there even two or three months beforehand, go to see the roads and the key points in the race.

SAUL: Wow, I always say preparation builds confidence, and that's certainly a great example.

CHRIS FROOME: Yeah, and quite often when I go and see these, I'll go see the finish climb of stage 10, or whatever it is, and I'll go and ride it once just to see it, and then I'll go back and ride it again at race speed just to really replicate at that kind of effort. So it basically leaves me with a really good picture of what exactly is required, so that's also going to help my training in the weeks leading up to the race so I know what kind of physical effort it's going to take.[37]

PEGGY: Similarly, in preparation for winning the Olympic road race, Nicole Cooke flew all the way to Beijing, China, the year before, to reconnoiter the road course. Then she prepared specifically for that route, simulating it physically and reinforcing success with mental rehearsal. Thorough preparation like that is a trademark of champions. I also prefer to mentally rehearse in great detail. The following coaching on mental rehearsal and scripting reflects my detailed approach to preparation. Knowing yourself and what works for you makes a difference here. If there is too much detail for you, feel free to skip over these examples and exercises, or come back to them at another time.

> If you want to try this detailed exercise, imagine, for example, a cross-country mountain bike race. You have seen the course, and you have clear memory of it. Picture it in your mind. Picture the start. You want to get off to a good start, to generate some speed and jump, and if possible, to get away from the pack. Imagine building up a charge just before the race starts. Imagine straddling your bike at the start line, breathing, turning the wheel, and generating some power. As the race starts, imagine yourself spinning with power and speed. You aren't forcing it. Now, it's an attack situation, but you stay relaxed as you draw in power and send it down and out, turning the wheel, picking up speed. You are the tiger. You are sprinting. You have good power. You are driving your legs. As you get farther away with that first group, you begin to scan the terrain, eyes open; you read the terrain and your position. You are in the lead group. You are beginning to smooth things out. You start to lower your heart rate. You want to pace yourself. Attack becomes smooth. You anticipate aspects of the course, see them, and react

smoothly, shifting gears, having a good feel through the rough spots, accelerating and attacking as the course demands or dictates. Visualize yourself riding the course as you want to, as you anticipate it, through a rocky section, smoothing it, being one with your bike–like a mountain lion tracking through the gnarly area with good control–controlling speed and direction with your brakes. You are handling the bike well, being at one with your bike. Create a mental picture of the course on which you will be riding. Make notes and sketches, if that helps you. Note the rough spots, then imagine you are smoothing it out and handling the bike through these challenging sections with more touch and feel. Note the flats and the areas with speed potential. Imagine moving into these flatter parts, anticipating, turning the wheel, attacking, and generating speed. Finish visualizing your ride with the most effort on the final lap. Finish feeling good about your ride.

CYCLE WISDOM

"Visualization provides extra training without the physical exertion. And believing that it is going to help is key. My teammate (Georgia Simmerling, the first Canadian to compete in three different sports in three different Olympic Games) told me she used it, so I thought I'd give it a try. Visualization builds confidence by allowing you to deliberately plan a race, and then imagine yourself doing it. I use two types of visualizing to prepare for a team pursuit. I view the standing start from my own eyes, focusing on the black line into the first turn. I see the exchanges as if watching a video of the whole team. I see myself go up the banking and drop down onto the last wheel precisely."

—Erin Attwell, Canada, Pan Am Games Medalist in Team Pursuit[38]

PEGGY: While mental rehearsal is useful in all kinds of cycling, it may be most important in downhill mountain biking. Downhill mountain bikers must have a clear mental picture of the course and mentally rehearse the entire course prior to the race so that they can see it clearly in their minds. In working with a downhiller, I usually begin by highlighting the difficult areas first, helping them to see themselves handling those sections well. Next, I encourage them to see themselves getting off to a good start, smoothing, anticipating the rough spots and handling them with ease. I ask them to identify the feelings they want to have, deciding where they are going to push down and where they are going to go around a boulder, anticipating, then seeing the speed sections where they can attack and generate even more speed. Linking these pieces together helps the racer see the course the way they want to experience it. Mental rehearsal is as important as physical practice for optimal cycling. Sometimes people don't actually perform the physical skills correctly. The skill tips I have outlined in Exercise 4.2 are fundamental. To improve your cycling, it's important to execute these skills properly and mentally rehearse doing them correctly.

EXERCISE 4.2

Rehearsing Skills

Visualize yourself doing skills required for your event. Picture having good form on the bike.

Flat Terrain

- Looking ahead
- Keeping elbows low and loose
- Shoulders relaxed
- Quickness in your legs

- Equal pedal strokes on each side making smooth strokes
- Increasing cadence and gearing to go faster

Cornering

- Looking ahead to where you want to be when exiting the turn
- Leading with your eyes, looking at the front of the pack
- Carrying speed and momentum though the turns effortlessly
- Letting go of the brakes
- Taking the best lines to maintain speed
- Jumping out of the turn to increase speed

Climbing seated

- Sitting up tall, opening up your breathing
- Hands on top of the bars
- Pulling back on the bars with every pedal stroke, right, left
- Pushing down on the pedals, using torso, quads, hamstrings, and calves

Climbing standing

- Preparing by selecting a gear
- Moving hands into position to stand
- Standing with weight over the bottom bracket
- Feeling the nose of your seat brushing the back of your legs
- Pulling up, pushing down with legs and feet
- Using your whole body like one smooth machine

Descending

- Looking ahead
- Using gravity and momentum to carry speed
- Keeping legs loose and moving
- Tucking your upper body

Tactically

- Drinking, eating when able
- Scanning the terrain and the pack, checking who is where in the group, who is looking fresh, calculating who is working hard and who is resting
- Selecting portions of the course to test yourself and others (accelerating out of corners to see who is alert and matches you)
- Using wheels of other riders to move up
- Looking for opportunities to break away or make up time

Sprinting

- Selecting a landmark to start your sprint
- Looking for that landmark and the finish line, using peripheral vision to monitor the racers around you
- Shifting into your sprint gear and gripping the bars tighter, preparing for the effort
- Jumping out of the saddle, all your energy directed into pushing the pedals down as fast as you can
- Pulling against the handlebars for leverage
- Getting to top speed, every pedal stroke counts and you don't stop pedaling until you cross the line

---

For a long race, it is difficult to imagine the whole race. You can imagine parts of it, especially the most difficult sections or where you think key actions might take place. You can imagine challenging climbs, breaking away, coming out of a start gate, passing competitors on tight trails, being crafty and pacing yourself wisely, attacking and handling a gnarly section effectively. Imagine the significant parts of your event. Make sure you are confident in your skills. Write or speak out how to do each component.

Scripting

Chaining all these skill components together, along with smooth and attack cues, can form a useful script of an upcoming event.

CYCLE WISDOM

"For me, scripting is hugely important. I review race scenarios like counting sheep before sleep."

—Larry Towner, U.S.A., Masters Multi-Time, Multi-Discipline New Jersey State Champion, Coach[39]

PEGGY: The following is an example of a script for a mountain bike cross-country race.

- I am warming up alone, feeling calm and focused.
- I have already checked my equipment and have given my water bottles to the team manager for the feed zone.
- I am breathing rhythmically, revving up the engine with my legs. Now it's time to go to the start line, and I am looking forward to being in control at the start.
- I finish off my water bottle and replace it with a full one. I do deep breathing to relieve tension in the corral. I imagine myself racing a lap.
- Just before the gun goes off, I am alert. My crank is in position for the first power stroke, my elbows are bent, ready to stand and pull the bike under me.
- Bang. We are off, and I am clipped in, standing on the pedals, sprinting, and looking ahead. I sit down and continue the charge. We are into the single track now.

- I begin to breathe deeply to slow my heart rate and recover from the start effort. I am relaxing, sitting up tall to breathe.
- I am finding my rhythm, using the riders in front of me for pacing.
- I climb seated, standing on steeper sections. I pump my bike over bumps and rocks. This is fun. I love this.
- One more long climb. I can do it with ease.
- I shift at the top preparing for the descent, relax, and let the bike go, let the front wheel track itself. I stand up and use my hips to rebalance my bike and body over rough spots.
- In the fast section, I look farther ahead. I push into the base of bumps and float over the top.
- I have completed one lap, and I am going to smoothly ride out the second lap, paying attention to drinking and maybe eating.
- At the end of lap 2, I want to be no more than 5% slower than the first lap. I want to hold that pace.
- In lap 3, I focus even more on the task as I become tired. Breathing and recharging, I am going to pass others, picking my passing spots.
- I use the front brake to control speed and the back brake to control direction.
- In lap 4, I give all my effort on the sections I am good at. I am very alert on those that I have difficulty with.
- I remind myself to breathe, to use cue words, and to love the moment.
- I give an extra effort to pass others while looking like I am riding with ease.
- I am aware of my position and can pick up time with each pedal stroke. I am reeling them in.
- As I cross the finish line, I know I gave my best effort. I am pleased.

EXERCISE 4.3

Making a Script

Chain together power words, thoughts, affirmations, images, and skills to form your own script.

- Select a course or event for which you want to prepare mentally.
- Select the desired feelings, power words, thoughts, and affirmations that will help you perform well, that you have tested in training and know work for you.
- Select the skills that the course demands and tactics you think will improve your chances of having a good ride.
- Trace the course, match the skills and thoughts you will need in each section.
- Review the script, add thoughts as to when to *smooth* and when to *attack*.
- Imagine riding the course using all the cues and thoughts you have prepared.

Imagery is like a motion picture, and you are the director of that mental movie. Watching your own high-performance movies will help you excel. Here are five tips that will enhance your mental rehearsal and help you direct a high-quality experience.

Define What You Want

Uncertainty leads to confusion and stress. One way to increase success and reduce stress is to create clear images of what you want to do and how you want to do it. Stay tuned into these images. They are your personal GPS. In defining your ride, be specific. Write it down, type it. Do some constructive daydreaming. Project or stream your energy into the images you want to create.

Relax, Then Imagine

Whenever possible, release tension and do some conscious breathing before putting your creative imagination to work for you. As you do, the quality of your images will become stronger, clearer, and more positive. Just taking a moment or two to relax and breathe will make it easier for you to imagine yourself riding at your best. In cycling, that may mean being faster, more powerful, riding with ease, making good strategy reads, having great jump, and finishing strongly.

Stay Positive

You will get more of what you imagine. Stay focused on the image of you at your best. The only value of running a negative thought or image, something that didn't work, is to determine what you can do to change it and enhance your cycling performance and pleasure. Once you are clear about that, mentally rehearse the positive.

Be Dynamic And Brief

Create imagery that is a dynamic movie, not a snapshot. Most riders find their imagery works best if they imagine the ride from the perspective of being the rider on the bike—what you see from your own eyes or as if you had a helmet cam. Others visualize as if they are a spectator watching themselves perform or being filmed by someone else as in a YouTube video. Try both approaches and see what works best for different sections.

Use All Your Senses

Make your mental rehearsal multi-sensory. Most people are strongly visual, and many think imagery is simply visual. Cycling has very strong visual, tactile, and kinesthetic elements. Incorporate all the sensory cues into your mental rehearsal. See it, feel it, hear it, and when appropriate, smell and taste it.

SAUL: Imagination is more powerful than the will. Your images are a blueprint that shape your performance. See it. Believe it. Do it.

HOMEWORK

Imagery

Practice is essential to incorporate the imagery suggestions presented in this chapter.

1. Continue to work with power thoughts and affirmations. Select eight of your favorites, and use them in training and racing to evaluate their effectiveness.
2. Create the image of your successful end result. It is important to have a picture of what you are striving for. Put a representation—a picture or drawing—of that image up on your wall or somewhere in front of you, where you can see it. Put that image in your mind. Clarifying intention is very empowering. Projecting and reflecting on that image can support and energize

you to carry on and realize your goal or dream. Every once in a while, sit back and imagine having achieved that goal. What the mind can conceive and believe, it can achieve. Feel it, see it, believe it, and do it.

3. Think of an animal that gives you the qualities that you would like to bring to your ride. Pick an animal that appeals to you and that you find stimulating. The big cats are popular because of their speed, agility, quickness, strength, and beauty. Wolves are popular because of their ability to hunt and run on their own and in a pack. Allow yourself to experience an awakening of your animal instinct. It can stimulate your cycling and provide a rich power source to be tapped. Work hard and have fun.
4. Create a script of a course you know and can imagine. Then mentally rehearse the elements of the script. Practicing this is extremely important. Visualize yourself being smooth and expertly handling difficult sections. Imagine yourself with good acceleration in the speed zones. See yourself being in control, being the boss, eyes open, making good decisions, anticipating, and executing well.

In this section (Chapters 2, 3, and 4), we covered managing your mind with Right Focus. Take charge in managing your mind. When you don't like what mental program is running, shift your focus. You have the power to shift to another mental program. Just like shifting gears on your bike is a fundamental skill, the skill of shifting focus is fundamental too. Choose to be more positive, to feel better, and to perform better.

RIGHT FEELING

In this section (Chapters 5 and 6), we emphasize the importance of creating Right Feeling, specifically feelings of power and ease, and how to use breathing to enable you to do that. Cycling success is about managing feelings. Remember, our feelings affect our thinking, and our thoughts affect our feelings. You can't maintain Right Focus without managing feelings of fear, frustration, anger, pain, and fatigue. As we stated repeatedly, you are the boss when it comes to how you think, feel, and act. Cycle Psyched is about tuning into winning programs. It's about creating and training Right Focus and Right Feeling.

CHAPTER 5
Managing Emotions & Conscious Breathing

Managing Emotions

Cycling is an intense, highly competitive, high-speed sport. To compete successfully, you must be able to manage your emotions and create Right Feeling. That means not only being able to energize, pump up, and attack, but also to calm down, regain composure, and be smooth. Many racers struggle with maintaining the right attack-smooth balance. The exact balance point varies depending on a rider's personality, talent, experience, event, and in some cases, their role on the team.

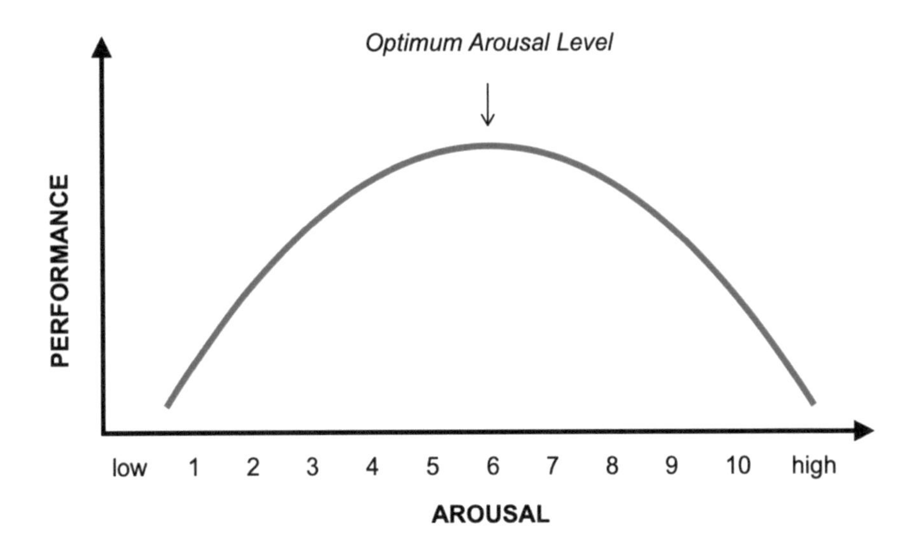

As you can see in the figure above, a low level of emotional intensity results in low performance. As the athlete becomes more engaged, performance improves to an optimum point. With more intensity, the athlete becomes over-aroused, and performance decreases.

SAUL: Most cyclists I have consulted with think they are at their best in the range of 6-8. What is important to understand is that if your emotional intensity is very low (3-4) you have to pick it up, draw in power, and then attack mentally. On the other hand, a more common problem is having emotional intensity that is above your optimal level, which leads to trying too hard, tensing, and feeling tight. In this case, conscious breathing can help you calm your emotions. For more intensity, the key word is *attack*. For more calm, the key word is *smooth.* Remember, you are the boss. You have the response-ability to control your feelings.

CYCLE WISDOM

"Actually, I was this morning super, super relaxed, and that made me a bit nervous because I was so relaxed. I was like, 'Oh, I need to wake up,' because you also need to have those nerves for a time trial, because it's good. In the end, if you have those nerves, you can really dig deep. Also, it makes you sharp. So this morning, I was first really relaxed, and then I got a bit nervous that I was so relaxed, and then the nerves came a bit, and I was good (in the end)."

—Demi Vollering, The Netherlands, Tour de France Femmes Winner[40]

CYCLE WISDOM

"Cycling demands physical capacity, robustness, and mental resilience. It's important to understand we need these packages put together. We work on these pieces. That's what it takes to build a champion. You understand you have God-given gifts...and you have gaps. A lot of preparation has been directed at shoring up those gaps. So that you become more well-balanced and a more complete athlete...not just where the heart, lungs, and legs are involved...but also between the two ears."

—Paulo Saldanha, Canada, Cycling Coach, Creator of PowerWatts, ISN World Tour Cycling Team Performance Director[41]

SAUL: Two questions I am frequently asked: "How do I know what number I am on the performance arousal scale? And what should I be?" Take some time to tune in, and become aware of how you feel when you are cycling at your best. At other times, check if what you are experiencing is more or less than that desired level of feeling; use your breathing and thinking to adjust. It's important to develop emotional control not just for race mastery, but also for staying strong and alert over a long racing season. If a rider is feeling nervous and stressed much of the time, they will burn out. One has to learn to manage emotions to stay healthy and energized. And conscious breathing is key.

CYCLE WISDOM

"When you get to key points, the pressure really builds up inside you. I'd say it's more about the pressure you put on yourself. Sometimes, in the excitement of the moment, you can get lost and maybe go off a little."

—David Gaudu, France, La Vuelta a España and Critérium du Dauphiné Stage Winner, 4th in GC Tour de France[42]

Conscious Breathing

Two things happen when you focus on your breathing.

1. Conscious breathing helps you to focus on the present moment. When athletes feel anxious and worried, it's usually about the future (e.g., What will happen if I perform poorly, miss an opportunity, embarrass myself, etc.). Frustration, on the other hand, lives in the past, when athletes become preoccupied with

mistakes made and opportunities squandered. The power is in the present. NOW is where the action is. Focusing on breathing brings your conscious mind into the here-and-now present. If you find yourself stuck worrying about the past or the future, take a breath and bring your attention back to this breath…back to the now.

2. Conscious breathing integrates mind and body. Most performance problems are the result of a disconnect between thoughts (your mind) and feelings (your body); mind and body are not in synch. It's as though these two parts are operating at different speeds. Frequently, the mind seems to be racing while the body lags behind. Conscious breathing allows you to integrate your thoughts and feelings.

CYCLE WISDOM

"Breathing is definitely a massive one. I think breathing is still not understood 100%, nor are the benefits you can get through breathing exercises. I've certainly found in warming up for a time trial, taking some deep breaths, slowing the breaths down really helps. It helps me to focus on what I really need to do...and it knocks everything else out."

—Chris Froome, Great Britain, 4x Tour de France Champion[43]

Our brains consist of two halves: the left and right cerebral cortices. The left hemisphere of the brain processes logical, analytic, and technical information. The right hemisphere of the brain deals more with feeling and coordination. It is more spontaneous and generates the feeling of making the right moves.

Left Hemisphere	**Right Hemisphere**
Feeling	Thinking
Intuitive	Analytic
Spontaneous	Planning
Present	Past or Future
Images	Words

Cycling success requires smooth, integrated functioning between the left and right cerebral hemispheres, between feeling and focus. It's about knowing what to do and doing it. It's about the left brain thinking clearly but not too much. It's about the right brain managing feelings and not letting strong emotions skew focus. Optimal performance occurs when the two halves of the brain perform in a coordinated and integrated fashion. Smooth, conscious breathing is one of the simplest and most effective ways to facilitate that coordination and contribute to a high-performance state. Cycle Psyched is about having focus, power, and emotional control. Conscious breathing is a key to all three.

CYCLE WISDOM

"Basic physical strength is necessary. The body, legs, muscles have to be there. But you stay on bikes for hours and hours, so you need to have a little imagination. You need to be intelligent and calm. You need mental control. It is self-control."

—Felice Gimondi, Italy, Grand Tour Triple Winner: Giro d'Italia, Tour de France, La Vuelta España.[44]

SAUL: What follows is a simple breathing process that is basic to generating Right Feeling and managing emotions. It is one of the most important performance-enhancing techniques I use. The three keys to conscious breathing are:

1. Rhythm
2. Inspiration (Inbreath)
3. Direction

In the following exercises–and in life–whenever possible, I recommend you breathe slowly and smoothly, and through your nose. It is the most efficient way to absorb oxygen. I suggest you practice the exercises every day. There is scientific evidence to confirm that if you regularly practice your breathing for 5-6 minutes a day, you will develop the capacity, even under pressure, to simply take a breath (or two) and be able to feel more calm, powerful, and in control.

After reading through the below processes a couple of times, we suggest you record the exercises on your phone or tablet. That way, you can play it back to yourself, relax, and really experience the process without having to read it.

EXERCISE 5.1

Rhythm

Perhaps the most important part of breathing is simply tuning into the rhythm of your breath. To get into your breathing rhythm, sit back, and relax.

Feel the inbreath come in...
And feel the outbreath go out...

Again, feel the inbreath come all the way in...
And feel the outbreath go all the way out...

The key to rhythm is time.
Give yourself time for the inbreath to come all the way in...
Give yourself time for the outbreath to flow all the way out...

Now, place one hand on your abdomen and one on your chest.
Notice as you breathe in...the abdomen and chest rise.
As you breathe out...they fall.
The breath is like waves in the ocean.
And you can always find the waves.

Give yourself time and feel the inbreath, the in-wave flowing in.
Give yourself time and feel the outbreath, the out-wave flowing out.
It is very simple. There is power in simplicity.

Experience the subtle power in connecting to your natural rhythm. It's a way in which we take control.

Inspiration (inbreath)

Once you have tuned into your breathing rhythm, the second key to focus on is the inspiration, or inbreath. Inspiration means to take in spirit. Your breathing is a source of energy and spirit.

Again, tune into your breathing.
Experience a nice smooth rhythm.
Give yourself time for the inbreath to come all the way in...
Give yourself time for the outbreath to flow all the way out...

As you breathe, place a little more emphasis on the inbreath.
Feel yourself drawing in energy with each breath you take.
You have a personal connection to an unlimited supply.

Again, feel yourself gently pulling in energy with each inbreath.
On the outbreath, allow yourself to release and relax.

Some cyclists have found it useful to think of inbreathing fresh, charged energy, and exhaling used energy and lactic acid.

To Continue

Experience a nice smooth breathing rhythm…
Feel yourself breathing in energy.

Hands: Now, on the outbreath, imagine energy flowing down through your shoulders and arms, into your hands.

Again, imagine breathing in energy, and on the outbreath, send, allow, and direct energy to flow down through your shoulders and arms, into the palms of your hands.

One more time, feel yourself drawing in, breathing in energy.
Again, allow yourself to imagine energy flowing down your arms and into your hands.

Feet: Now, imagine yourself breathing in energy, and this time, on the outbreath, allow energy to flow down your legs, into your feet.

Again, feel yourself breathing in energy.
On the outbreath, allow that energy to flow down your quads and calves, and into the soles of your feet.
Feel the energy in the soles of your feet.
It is always a smooth breathing rhythm…like waves in the ocean.
Breathing in energy and sending it out.
Allowing it to flow down your arms and your hands…strong hands.
Down your legs and your feet…cat's feet.
Eyes: Okay, once again, experience a smooth breathing rhythm…

breathing in energy. This time as you breathe out, imagine energy flowing up your spinal column, into your head and eyes.

Now, close your eyes, and allow the place behind your eyes to relax. As you relax and breathe, feel energy flowing to you and through you. Out to your hands, feet, and eyes…like a five-pointed star.

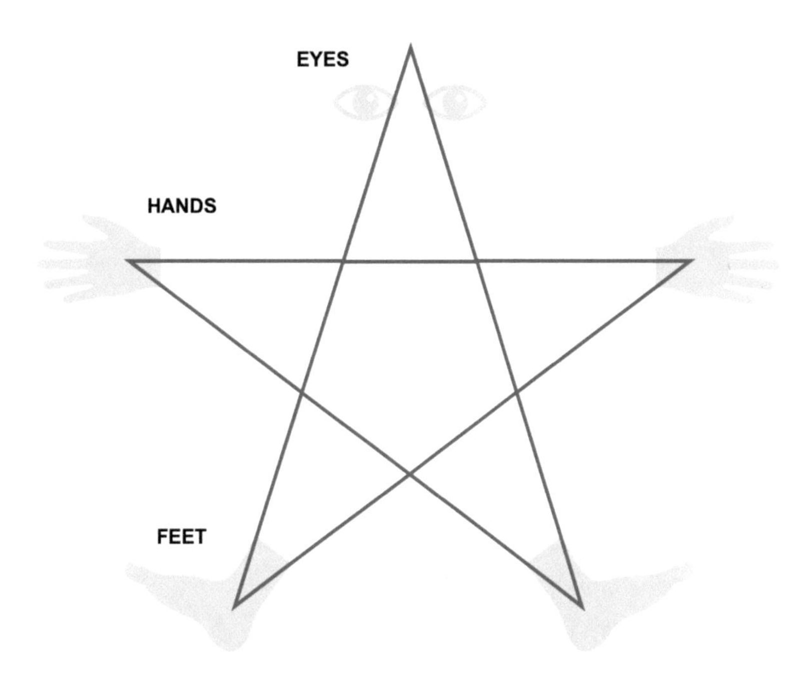

Feel the energy flow to your hands, feet, and eyes, like a five-pointed star.

As you relax and breathe, know that you are a good cyclist.
Think of your strengths, three to four reasons why you are good.
Imagine yourself racing with power, ease, and speed.
With excellent form and control.
See it. Feel it.
Good.
For the next 4–5 minutes, simply relax and breathe.

CYCLE WISDOM

"Saul, thinking about how you have helped me over the years reminded me of a story well after we had been working together and how breathing and visualization indirectly won me an Olympic silver medal. It was right before my most successful day as a cyclist, the night before I won my medal. I awoke bright eyed at 3 am. I was ready to go!! I knew I had to get back to sleep, but I was anxious and ready to race. There was nothing in the room to relax me, so I read the only thing handy, yesterday's USA Today Sports section of the newspaper. I thought I'd read all the box scores of games. That should put me to sleep! After 15 minutes, still no luck feeling sleepy. I had to shut off the lights and at least try to fall asleep. I turned off the lights, closed my eyes, and began visualizing the waves gently rolling into the shore and back out again. I counted the breaths entering and leaving my body, relaxing energy in, anxiety out. I don't remember even making it to 10 breaths and woke up at 8 am, energized and ready to take on the world!"

—Brian Walton, Canada, Olympic Points Race Silver Medalist, Founder of Walton Endurance, Corporate Cycling Experiences[45]

PEGGY: Having good breath control will help immensely in emergency situations, like when you have had a close call with traffic buzzing you, or if you do experience a tragedy and are in pain. Deep, controlled breathing can prevent the situation from getting worse. This applies across all sports.

In PGA champion Curtis Strange's words: "Under pressure one of the most important things I have to remember, is to breathe."[46]

EXERCISE 5.2

Tension Release

The next part of managing feelings has to do with being better able to release tension. Tension can be a tiring and limiting drag.

Sit back, relax, and breathe.
Experience how your body feels.
Now, we'll experience the contrasting feelings of tension and release.

Hands
Create tension in your hands by making tight fists.
Squeeze your fists and bend your wrists in.
Hold for five seconds.
Feel the tension.
Now let it go. Just let it drop.
Release. And after you release, take a breath.

Experience (and practice) that feeling of releasing and breathing. People rarely hold a lot of tension in their hands unless they are angry, anxious, or frustrated. However, because we are very familiar with our hands, the hands are an excellent place to begin exploring the tension-release process.

Shoulders
Next, focus your attention on your shoulders.
Raise your shoulders up three or four inches.
Hold and feel the tension there. The neck and shoulders are primary tension holding areas.
Let go. Release and breathe.
Always release and breathe.
This time, raise your shoulders up one inch.

The tension is hardly detectable, but you can still feel it.
Notice that you restricted your breathing and limited its power.
Hold for five seconds.
Now release your shoulders.
Take a breath.
Always release and breathe.

From time to time, check your body for tension. Remember to release the tension and breathe.

Chest and Abdomen

As you relax and breathe, place one hand on your abdomen and one on your chest.
Feel these parts of your body expand and contract with each breath you take.
The breath is like waves in the ocean.
Feel the waves rise and fall with each breath.
Allow your abdomen and chest to be free to expand and contract with each breath you take.

Pubic Area

Now, focus your attention on the genitals. The genitals are a primary tension area.
Squeeze the sphincter muscle that you tighten when you hold back from using the toilet.
As you squeeze that muscle, notice it affects your breathing.
Hold for five seconds.
Then release and breathe.
Always release and breathe.

Feet

Finally, curl your toes, making fists with your feet.
It is like a bird gripping a branch.
Feel the tension and hold for five seconds.

Now let it go.
Release and take a breath.
Remember, whenever you feel tension, always release and breathe.

You can tense or release any part of your body. You are the boss. You are in control. What is important is that you learn how to scan your body, feel where you have tension, and let it go. Then go back to the power source which is breathing. The release reflex involves awareness, release, and breathing. It is the key to releasing unnecessary tension and managing your emotions well.

SAUL: Again, success in bicycle racing, and in life, is about learning how to manage your mind. A key to managing your mind is being able to release tension and negativity and generate feelings of calm and power in any situation. Then it's about focusing your energies on what you want to make happen.

PEGGY: Let me give you an example. In mountain bike racing and cyclocross, riders sometimes crash just after completing a difficult section of the course, whether it's a hard climb or a slippery downhill. They have just worked very hard, and they are tired. It's as if they let up and lose focus and control after they have completed the short-term challenge. If they simply focus on maintaining a smooth breathing rhythm, they would be better able to stay focused and in control, and these let-down incidents would be less likely to happen.

Another example of using breathing to perform well is when you need to slow down in order to make good choices. What if you get to a race and discover you have left some essential piece of equipment, such as your helmet, at home? Your heart starts pounding, you are breathing rapidly, your palms are sweaty. By relaxing and taking a breath instead of panicking, you may be able to come up with some intelligent solutions such as finding a friend in another category to borrow from, locating the nearest bike shop, or going home to get your helmet. As a coach, I have been faced with time-pressured situations like this, and being calm has helped both me and my riders deal with these challenges effectively.

An elite mountain bike racer related how this happened to her in a World Cup event. She was getting ready to start the race and realized that she had left her race number in the condo where she was staying. Her team mechanic knew the condo and ran off to get the number. However, the seconds were ticking away. With less than five minutes to go, the racer was at the start line. With less than one minute to go she was lined up, and the mechanic was pinning on her number. She rode an excellent race. Afterward, she said what had helped her keep it together was the mechanic, and remembering to breathe smoothly.

In the exercises, we describe our simple, effective technique for creating feelings of calm and power. As you breathe smoothly and rhythmically, you will use your energy more effectively, feel lighter, and have less fatigue. And you will be better able to control your feelings.

EXERCISE 5.3

Conscious Breathing & Racing

All right, let's go through it again, this time in a cycling scenario.

Relax and breathe.
As you do, feel yourself drawing in energy.
Experience energy flowing through you, like a star.
Now, allow yourself to imagine that you are on your bicycle.

Imagine that you are riding with smoothness and power.
You have good form.
You are drawing in energy.
Energy is flowing through you.
You have strength through your glutes and quads.
You are spinning, turning over the pedals with ease.
Your upper body is relaxed.
You are feeling good.
Feel energy flowing up your spinal column, flowing up into clear eyes. You can see clearly.
You are breathing easily, you are riding with ease and power.
You have great form and are feeling good.
If you are holding tension, don't drag it around with you. Let it go.
Draw in energy.
Experience energy flowing through your body.
Think about yourself as a star.
Imagine riding with smoothness and power.
Release and breathe.

Enjoyment is the foundation to optimal cycling. One of the keys to being a successful cyclist is to enjoy riding your bicycle. It is your response-ability to create feelings of ease and power, and to shift your energy into technique and form on the bicycle.

CYCLE WISDOM

"In calm moments and even when I'm training, I always think of taking full breaths. I'll be doing a core workout, and when it's hard, I'll sometimes forget to breathe…then I realize I'm holding my breath, and I get back into breathing. In moments of high stress, I'm not always thinking about breathing, but if the race is just going along, then I think about my heart rate, breathing smoothly, and experiencing a long exhale."

—Benjamin Perry, Canada, UCI World Tour Pro[47]

Empowerment

The beginning of being empowered is being mindful of your breathing and drawing in energy. Then sending or allowing that energy to flow through your total being.

SAUL: A woman named Gail came to see me prior to her road race at an important international Games. It was late in her season which included success in the grueling Tour de France Féminine. When I met her she was tired, and after 20 hours of travel, she didn't feel much like racing in the hot, humid weather of the tropics. To make matters worse, along with jet lag and fatigue, she had strained a muscle in a training ride, and she was hurting. Since feelings affect thinking, it's not surprising that Gail's fatigue and unease were contributing to her thinking less-than-positive thoughts. I listened to her describe her feelings for a few minutes. Then we began to work with her breathing, with rhythm and inspiration. Within a few minutes, she began to feel more comfortable and more powerful. As she felt more powerful, her confidence grew. We had two sessions before the road race. Gail rode a good race finishing at the head of the field and supporting her teammate who won the gold medal. Forty-eight hours after the road race was another grueling challenge, the time trial. Again, the feelings of fatigue and unease began to play and reduce Gail's power and confidence. Again, we spent several sessions focusing on her breathing, on rhythm, inspiration, and streaming energy out like a five-pointed star. As she did, she began to feel empowered. Then we added some positive race imagery to the good feelings, and Gail was ready to go. And go she did, winning a silver medal in the Games.

Just as this world-class racer used breathing to empower herself, and the rider at the start line used breathing to calm down, anyone affected by the stresses of daily life can use breathing to recharge and prepare for a challenging ride. Indeed, many of the examples in this training program are of competitive and elite cyclists because they frequently perform under intense pressure. However, the technique that we describe is simple and useful for everyone.

EXERCISE 5.4

Power Up

Power is a force that will work for you. Use your breathing to turn the wheel with power.

> *Breathing is the key to filling yourself with energy and power.*
> *Tap the mains. Draw in the energy.*
> *Take three deep breaths.*
> *Let energy flow through you…and build.*

SAUL: At the Pan American Games in Caracas, Venezuela, I was consulting with several teams. As part of a three-hour, intensive training program, I introduced several bike racers to a breathing technique to give them more power, endurance, and ease. Included in the group was Damian, a 21- year-old road racer, a tall kid with curly blond hair and a baby face. He was scheduled to be racing the 200 km road race over the hot, hilly countryside the following day.

A couple of hours after the race, Damian approached me. "You know, Dr. Miller, that breathing stuff you were teaching us the other day is great. It really works." I asked what made him say that. "Well, about 60 kilometers into the race, I started to get really woozy. I guess I hadn't hydrated sufficiently, and I began to feel as though I might pass out. Then I remembered that breathing technique that you taught us…and I started to do it." Damian paused. "You know, I went another 20 kilometers before I passed out." I often mention to clients I know that if I would go to the gym and lift weights, I would get stronger. But I don't go to the gym. Knowing this information and understanding it just isn't enough. To acquire the ability to manage your emotions under pressure, you have to actually do this conscious breathing and tension-release training, repeatedly.

HOMEWORK

We strongly encourage you to be diligent about your practice of these assignments.

1. Do Exercises 5.1 and 5.2 (approximately 10 minutes per day)
2. Once per day, after breathing and relaxing, imagine yourself riding with:

    - Smoothness
    - Power
    - Ease
    - In slow motion
    - Power, speed, and excellent form
3. On the bike, experiment with how breathing rhythm works best for you in different situations, for example, while climbing, time trialing, or recovering.
4. Keep a journal of your findings in this mental training process, recording your thoughts and feelings. This is private, so you can be entirely honest with yourself.
5. Try the following brain-balancing exercise for 10 days
    - Trace a lemniscate with your finger or eyes.

In this second section, we began working on Right Feeling, the second key to mental strength after Right Focus. We introduced conscious breathing; using breathing to relax, to generate power, and to direct that power. In the next chapter, we continue to use breathing as a tool to effectively manage our emotions.

CHAPTER 6
Changing Mental Programs

It is important to be able to create good feelings; to relax and breathe, to feel energy flowing through your body. It is also important to be able to change a tense, anxious, negative thought into a positive feeling.

"Accept, adapt, and move on," is a mantra repeated by Annemiek van Vleuten who has won over 100 pro races, for dealing with a flat, a crash, or the unexpected. "You can get really angry about a flat tire, but you cannot do anything about it, and it's better to make the best out of it…the same with a broken elbow. I was last year thinking like, 'okay, I can still help Marianne Vos [her teammate] to become World Champion. So let's start the race and at least go home with a better feeling.' That was my mentality last year with my broken elbow [sustained during the team relay event at the World Championships]. Then I got [to be] World Champion." Van Vleuten continued, "You need to make the best out of it…accept, adapt, and move on."[48]

Annemiek van Vleuten

The Release Reflex

Saul: When I share the Cycle Psyched message with cycling groups, I emphasize the importance of positive thinking, high-performance imagery, managing the emotions, and having a winning attitude. One question I am frequently asked by athletes refers to a genuine concern for many: "When I'm feeling really upset or frustrated, what can I do to get out of that negative feeling space?" Swearing, getting pissed off, or hanging one's head does nothing to move things forward. In fact, since we get more of what we think about, it often only highlights the negative. The real questions are: "How can I quickly and effectively change my feelings?" and "Is there a mechanism for changing programs on my mental computer?" There is. It's the release reflex, and it's based on the conscious breathing and tension release processes we introduced in the previous chapter.

The release reflex is remarkably simple. Whenever you feel anxiety, negativity, tension, or frustration: release…breathe in…refocus.

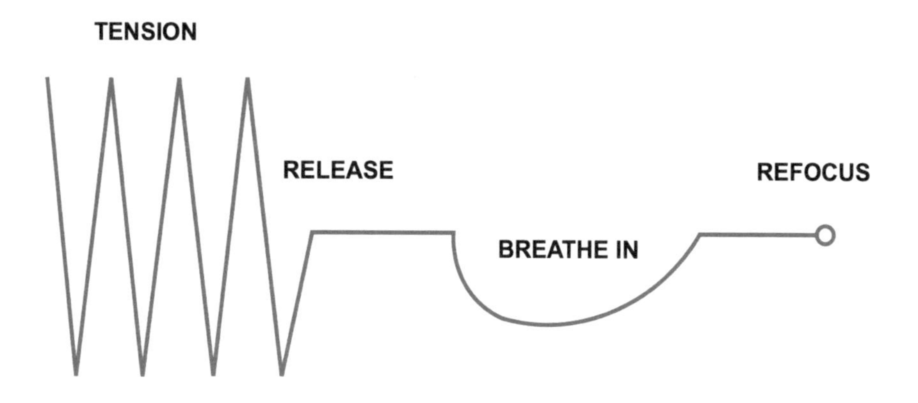

The Release Reflex Process

SAUL: I usually introduce the release reflex after running through the conscious breathing process (rhythm, inspiration, and direction). In Exercise 6.1, we will extend the tension release process we introduced in Chapter 5, and relate it to eliminating limitations and changing programs on your mental computer.

EXERCISE 6.1

The Release Reflex

This process has six steps.

1. To begin, make tight fists and feel the tension between the fingers and in the center of your hands. Turn your wrists inward

and hold it for five seconds. Now release the tension and breathe in. That ability to release tension and take a breath is key. Remember, always release and breathe.

2. Next, raise your shoulders up to your ears. Feel the tension associated with that and notice how it hinders breathing. Hold it five seconds, then release the tension and breathe in. Again, be aware of that feeling of letting go. Always release and breathe.
3. Now, raise the shoulders just one inch. The tensing is almost imperceptible to others, but you can feel it, and it impedes breathing. Hold it for five seconds. Then release and breathe. Again, understand it is always release and breathe.
4. Now, imagine someone directing a punch at your face. You see it coming, and you duck. It's a reflex. It's automatic. Then take a breath. Consciously, breathe in energy.
5. Now, imagine an opposing rider coming right up to you, with his/her face just eight inches from your face, saying something threatening or challenging. It's a verbal assault—not a physical one. Again, it triggers a defensive fight or flight reflex. Immediately, you tense up. Release and breathe.
6. This is what we have been building up to, whenever you experience a negative, anxious, or frustrated thought, it will trigger the same tensing reaction. The solution or response to that tensing reflex is: RELEASE the tension…BREATHE in…and REFOCUS on something positive.

With release, there is an exhalation. The breathing in action that follows, sharpens the arousal system and primes it for positive input. Then input the positive thought.

Again, what is important to understand is that for an instant, the release and breathe in process will clear the screen on your mental computer and release the tension, anxiety, or negativity you are experiencing. Then you have to refocus and introduce a positive thought (something like, *I'm okay, I can handle this, turn the wheel, be the hunter*), or visualize a positive image.

The release reflex is key to mental management. It is the way to clear the screen on your mental computer. It involves first being aware of tension, anxiety, frustration, and negativity, then letting it go, breathing in energy, and refocusing on something positive. Use negative experience and transform it into something positive. Remember, feelings affect thinking, and you are the boss.

The example described earlier in Chapter 3 of the four TTT riders knocking 15 and a half minutes off the Canadian record, is a good example of using both the release reflex and power words. Whenever these riders experienced a negative, anxious, or painful thought or feeling like, *it's too fast* or *I can't keep this up*, and they realized what they were thinking, they were able to release the tension, breathe in energy, and refocus on their power word.

PEGGY: I learned a similar technique from a psychologist I worked with early on in my career while racing for Team U.S.A. She would ask me to visualize a race and share aloud my inner commentary. When Dr. Berkowitz heard a negative, like, *oh no, here comes a climb*, she would yell, *STOP*. It was shocking at first, but I did learn to take a breath, and come up with something positive to replace the tense, anxious, or negative thought, and carry on. The next step was for me to stop myself when I recognized the negative self-talk. Eventually, I developed more positive and encouraging inner dialogue and refrained from the unhelpful thoughts while visualizing and while riding.

Learning how to deal with intense pressure and using the release reflex to change programs is a valuable skill for cycling…and in life.

Parking It

Some sport psychologists have used the concept *park it* to describe the experience of tuning out distracting, negative, or irrelevant thoughts, and staying tuned into what is appropriate. If a thought comes to mind that is not going to help you perform or can interfere with your cycling performance, *park it* and change programs.

SAUL: Cassie Campbell twice captained Team Canada to Olympic gold in hockey, and then became a broadcaster for the NHL. I asked Cassie, an experienced athlete and someone who observes sport at the highest level, what she thought was the most important mental quality for an athlete to acquire. "I think it's the ability to park it. Not to let any of the many possible distractions affect your performance. That ability enables a player to stay focused and follow through on what is asked of him or her."[49] Parking it requires perspective and emotional control, both aspects of mental toughness. Your ability to tune out a thought, change channels, and park it, is a combination of your motivation and your ability to release, breathe, and refocus. One of my favorite examples of mental discipline, and something I am fond of telling athletes, is: When I walk through my neighborhood and my neighbor's dog barks, I don't bark back. I have repeated this dozens of times. Usually, most athletes smile and nod. They can appreciate that if an opposing athlete barks at them, many athletes lose focus and almost reflexively bark back. My advice is, don't go there. Ignore it. Park it. If you do notice the provocation, use it, or it will use you.

How can you use it? As always, change the program, take a breath, release (anger, tension, fear, or whatever), and focus instead on the positive, on what you want to make happen. Mental toughness is about maintaining that positive focus, no matter what.

CYCLE WISDOM

"The key is to be able to endure psychologically."

—Greg LeMond, U.S.A., Pro Road World Champion, 3x Tour de France Winner[50]

SAUL: I spoke to Hugo Houle, a Tour de France stage winner, about how our feelings affect our thinking, and the feeling that limits us the most is fear: fear of failure, fear of embarrassment, fear of missing the break, fear of being dropped, fear of not being okay, fear of letting the team down. Fear is a contraction. The opposite of fear is love. Loving the challenge. Love is power. I asked Houle, "If you are feeling anxious, what do you do to change the feeling?"

HUGO HOULE: "I always try to remind myself it's just a game. I'm here to play. And, I can lose, it's not a problem. I do 80 races a year. Some are more important, others are less important. When it's more important, I tell myself okay, now it's time to go for it. And maybe I'll do fine. Maybe I crash, or puncture, but I know I'll give my best out there. And if the outcome is not good, what can I do? It is what it is. We can just let it go, analyze what we missed, and work to be better."[51]

CYCLE WISDOM

"The difference in racing at a high level like this is in your head.... How did you keep your cool with the pressure of this race? By controlling the things I can control, like my effort and where I want to be in the sprint. If you just stay calm, you'll stay in control and be able to analyze things. But if you freak out and think, 'Shit, I'm gonna mess up,' it's like you're already messing up in your head and you make wrong decisions. Keep it cool, keep it calm."

—Coryn Labecki, U.S.A., 73x National Champion, Tour of Flanders Winner[52]

CYCLE WISDOM

"It's made a huge difference to me to learn to let go of things I have no control over, and to shift my thinking to what I can control."

—Erin Attwell, Canada, Pan Am Games Team Pursuit Medalist[53]

When confronted with negativity, anxiety, frustration, or anger, release…breathe…refocus. Change channels. Park it and focus on cycling well.

PEGGY: Early in my racing career, I learned that if I was too verbal in races, it sometimes gave others the information that I might be frustrated or tired. If I kept calm and focused, I could make better use of a situation. In one race, my teammate was off the front. I had a world-class athlete on my wheel encouraging me to pull harder, to also break away from the group. I felt pressured but also thought she was manipulating me to drag her along, so I did some breathing and waited until she gave up on me. Then I attacked, left her in the dust, and soloed to second place, giving our team a 1–2 finish. That reinforced how beneficial it is to:

1. Be quiet and breathe more…breathe and reserve your energy.
2. Assess and use the situation to your advantage, channeling your energy.

SAUL: Breathing is like turning the wheel…as the wheel turns, it generates power.

EXERCISE 6.2

Turning The Wheel

You are a power generator.

Imagine your breath as a wheel.
As you breathe in, the wheel turns up.
As you breathe out, the wheel turns down.
Experience your breath as spinning the wheel.
As the wheel spins, it generates power.
Allow yourself to feel it.
Imagine breathing in energy and sending out power.
Now, imagine you are on your bike and you are riding with a group of people. It's a competition situation. As you ride, experience the feeling of smooth breathing; experience the feeling of turning the wheel and powering up.

Turning the wheel generates power. In the previous chapter, we noted that there were three things to focus on with breathing. The first is rhythm; the second is focusing on the inbreath; the third is directing energy out into your feet, hands, and eyes. The same thing applies to turning the wheel.

Alex Amiri commented that he applied the breathing wheel exercise in Exercise 6.2 to his training and riding while Everesting, i.e., completing consecutive hill repeats in a single session to equal the height of Mount Everest. Amiri found it helped keep his breathing smooth and purposeful, and he matched it with his pedaling technique. "I breathe a wheel—a wheel is round. You pedal in circles—also round. The mental-physical connection of thinking about breathing a wheel paired with pedaling in circles really helped me maintain rhythm for much longer than I anticipated."[54]

PEGGY: As cyclists, we have the idea of spinning built into us–turning the cranks, pushing the right pedal down while pulling up on the left, then down on the left, up on the right. As we spin, we can use the concept of generating power. Another fundamental of cycling, is shifting gears and changing speeds. When you are hurting, you can sometimes ease up or shift to a different gear. When you scan yourself physically and mentally, and feel you need to make a change, shift and spin the wheel!

EXERCISE 6.3

Sending Power Out

Let's try it again. Imagine riding, monitoring yourself, and deciding you should shift:

Feel yourself breathing in power, and then sending it out.
Imagine power flowing throughout your body.
Allow energy to flow down through your arms and into your hands.
Experience a firm grip, loose elbows, and relaxed shoulders.
Imagine that your upper body is quiet and energy is flowing through it.

This time, send the energy down, down though your hips, glutes, and quads…into your feet, into the power pads in the soles of your feet.

Imagine being on your bike and breathing, spinning the wheel.
Feel your hip and leg action like a big smooth wheel, spinning and generating power.
Draw in energy, send it down.
Imagine your hip and leg like a locomotive wheel, smoothly and easily powering your bike.
Breathe in energy...spin the wheel.
Send energy up into your eyes.
With eyes open, anticipate.
Read the terrain.
Read the riders.
Read the action of the race.
Feel your energy.

Feeling tired?
Use it...go deeper into your breathing.
Spin the wheel.
Generate power.

Send energy out like a five-pointed star.
Down into your legs: smooth, flowing, and spinning.
Send energy into your arms: relaxed shoulders, loose elbows, and firm hands.
Send energy into your eyes.
It's always eyes open, always aware, looking for the other strong wheels, and ready to jump...watching, and riding smart.

Now, imagine picking up the pace as you ride.
Begin to spin with a little more speed.
Imagine the feeling of quick feet, almost dancing on the pedals.

Imagine beginning to climb.
Go deeper into your breathing.

Spin the wheel and send more power down through the drive train.
Send power through your glutes and quads into your feet.
Imagine generating more power.
Feel that power driving the cranks.

Imagine picking up speed as you head up the incline.
Draw energy with the inbreath and send it down through the rest of your body.
As you send power down, the spin of the wheel is smooth and strong.

Now, imagine you are moving toward a flatter section, picking up more speed and using harder gears with more ease.
Imagine spinning the wheel and sending power through your hips and quads.
Imagine a continuous flow of energy as you breathe in.
And then exhale power into your lower body.
Spin the wheel with speed and ease…smoothly.

Always return to the idea of spinning the wheel.
It gives you energy.
Feel yourself breathing in energy.
Feel yourself spinning the wheel.

Imagine riding on the track. The track is really smooth and fast.
Imagine you are doing speed-work.
You are breathing, spinning the wheel, sending the energy down your legs, down like pistons, down, increasing your revolutions per minute.
You are quicker, lighter, and more streamlined. You are spinning the wheel faster, generating more speed, more rpms.
Imagine going faster than ever before.
Great.

A winning strategy for cycling and life is: whatever comes up, USE IT. In cycling, USE anxiety and doubt as a cue to release tension, breathe in energy, and use that energy to spin the wheel.

Eric Wohlberg was a successful international racer and a pragmatist. When consulting with Saul, he confided that he was a bit leery of sport psychologists. One of the problems he had had with a previous sport shrink was actually applying the advice he had received. Too much of it was complicated and difficult to use while riding under pressure. Understandably, if something is to be useful, it needs to be presented in a simple manner so it's easy to understand and put to use. Saul asked Eric if the idea of experiencing breathing as a wheel —spinning that wheel in order to generate more power, and then sending that power out—was simple and useful. "That's great," he replied. "That'll work." A couple of months later, Eric told Saul: "You know, I've got to tell you something. That breathing stuff really does work. I was using it in my weight training, and I found that it really increased my power and endurance lifting. It's just a matter of understanding how to use the generator idea while riding."[55]

PEGGY: You may need to transform the fatigue and stress reactions that arise when things go wrong in a race. Remember, you choose your response to a situation. Have you ever missed a feed during a race? Got a flat tire or mechanical? There are so many examples of riders having problems in races, handling them, and carrying on to win.

- Chantal Blaak crashed with under 40 km to go in the 2017 World Championships road race, got up, caught back on, got into a break with two favored teammates, attacked the break, and won solo.
- Elia Viviani and Mark Cavendish both crashed in the 2016 Olympic points race but went on to win gold and silver, respectively, in the omnium event.

- Connie Carpenter missed picking up a feed from the staff in the feed zone but nevertheless won the first ever women's road race in the Olympics.
- Clara Honsinger's team van carrying her race bike got a flat tire and was severely delayed in arriving at the Cyclocross National Championships course. She remained calm and won her first elite women's title.

There are also some spectacular examples of athletes not maintaining emotional control when things go wrong. *Cycling Weekly* republished an article showing "The Nine Best Bike Throws in the History of Cycling," as in tossing bikes after malfunctions or crashes. *Bobke TV*, Bob Roll's cycling show, also did a compilation of nasty bike tosses. While humorous, they show athletes who lost their composure and lost the race. As Roll himself says with a smile, "If you're riding your bike out there, and you get frustrated with it, and you don't have bike insurance…just calm down, take it easy, get the problem sorted and fixed, and avoid throwing the bicycle."[56]

Beware that as you cycle in any situation—on the road, trails, or on the track—whether you are feeling strong or tired, always use your situation or feelings as a stimulus or cue to remind you to spin the wheel. Increase the flow. Send the power out. There is energy flowing, and you are a five-pointed star.

Blowing Off Tension

Another way to use your breathing that will both increase intensity and reduce tension is something Saul borrowed from the martial arts. It involves doing some circular breathing—spinning the wheel—and then focusing the energy generated into a series of short punches, which are not directed at anyone. It's as though you are punching through a block of soft, corky wood. Each punch is accompanied by a deep-seated yell. There is a specific way to punch and yell that can be communicated with a little coaching. However, any series of six to eight short, crisp punches accompanied by a deep, inner-chest-centered yell (not throat centered) can be energizing and at the same time can blow off tension. The classic karate yell sound of *kiai* can be used, or you can use whatever sound feels right to you.

SAUL: Curt Harnett was a track cyclist famous for using this punch-and-yell routine to energize and blow off excess tension. He won an Olympic silver medal and set a world record in the flying 200 meter. This technique of circular breathing, punching, and yelling can be effective and fun. Try it. It is a great way to blow off pre-race tension. Then take a moment to breathe in energy to build up the charge. This blowing off tension and recharging is an effective, expressive way to use your breathing for a performance lift.

Curt Harnett using breathing to prepare for his Olympic performance.

PEGGY: I was startled when a competitor made noise–a loud noise–when initiating her final sprint at the Nutley, New Jersey, criterium. She was energizing and very focused, and her method distracted me. She won our two-up breakaway sprint. It highlighted to me how important it is to have a game plan for the final move and to have the consciousness to avoid being distracted. I planned my final sprint better the next day, visualized it, even adding some imaginary chaos, jumping first from the breakaway to win the U.S. National Criterium Championship at the Tour of Somerville. And what I did in the race was exactly as I had visualized it. If you practice it, visualize it, own it, your body will respond automatically. At any time, you can use breathing to recharge when you are tired. When I was a racer I met with Dr. Bruce Ogilvie on Friday afternoons in an office at a local fitness club in Los Gatos, California. I was usually very tired and would have normally napped during that time. Instead, we worked on recharging, which involved getting into my breathing, and then sending energy out through my body–like directing energy out to the five-pointed star. I have very vivid recollections of feeling the energy surge through my veins. In one session, I heard bolts of electricity shoot through my body, like lightening crackling across the sky. I was definitely reenergized.

There are seven energy centers or chakras. These chakras are located at the base of the spine; the sex organs; mid-torso; mid-chest; throat; in the middle of your forehead, which is also known as the third eye; and at the top of your head, i.e., the crown chakra. There are a number of yoga and meditation techniques that combine simple breathing with directing attention to these energy centers.

Work with your breathing. Be creative. Use your intuition to improve your experience. The ultimate test is how it feels and whether it works for you.

Mastering Pain

Again and again when we talk to a rider, pain comes up as a significant, limiting obstacle to optimal cycling. While every rider experiences some pain, we all have different pain thresholds. Learning to manage pain effectively is an important part of elite cycling.

CYCLE WISDOM

"I know the pain of cycling can be terrible—in your legs, your chest, everywhere. You go into oxygen debt and fall apart. Not many people outside of cycling understand that."

—Greg LeMond, U.S.A., Pro World Road Champion, 3x Tour de France Winner[57]

CYCLE WISDOM

"It's a mental game between the pain you feel in your legs and how bad you want it in your head.... Dealing with the pain is one of the biggest talents if you want to be a professional cyclist. Luckily, I like to hurt myself."

—Wout van Aert, Belgium, Cyclocross World Champion, World Road Championship Medalist[58]

CYCLE WISDOM

"Suffering is unavoidable. It is at the heart of racing. You have to suffer. You have to be able to get through what other people can't."

—Marc Madiot, France, 2x Winner of Paris–Roubaix, UCI WorldTeam Directeur Sportif[59]

CYCLE WISDOM

"To be a cyclist is to be a student of pain. Sure the sport is fun...but at cycling's core lies pain, hard and bitter as the pit inside a juicy peach. It doesn't matter if you are sprinting for an Olympic gold medal, a town sign, a railhead, or the rest stop with the homemade brownies. If you never confront pain, you are missing the essence of the sport."

—Scott Martin, U.S.A., Paralympic Road and Track Cyclist[60]

By mastering pain with training and using conscious breathing, you can reduce its power and be better prepared to stave it off longer. Pain is always there, and it can bring the best of riders to a halt, or it can help them set records.

While describing her Hour Record performance, French World Champion Catherine Marsal, explained how the experience taught her things she still uses in her professional life today.

> "To focus on the Hour was a learning process of understanding where your limits are, how much further you can go, how you can trick the mind to go through periods of discomfort. Some riders just get stuck in that pain zone, but if you can manage to get through that, everything flows. I learned there is a zone beyond that, which you can step into."[61]

Based on Saul's experience of operating an interdisciplinary pain clinic for several years and consulting with athletes, specifically cyclists, for over four decades, he has come up with insights that are useful for dealing with pain.

Pain Management

The three basic principles of mind management outlined in Chapter 1 are helpful to review:

1. The mind is like an amazing super computer. If you don't like what you are thinking or feeling, shift to another program. You are the boss.
2. You get more of what you think about. If you are thinking about pain, or how much you are hurting, or how painful it's going to be, you intensify the pain.
3. Feelings affect thinking, and thinking affects feeling. Again, pain is one of the major limiting programs experienced by elite cyclists. Pain causes tension, and tension increases pain. In addition, feeling pain can lead to limited and defensive thinking. Defensive thinking leads to more tension, contraction, dis-ease, and pain.

So how do we best deal with pain? The answer again is use it. The first and best pain-management skill is to create more ease. Shift the focus from feelings of pain, to your breathing rhythm, to spinning the wheel, to power thoughts and performance images. Use pain as a stimulus and a reminder to refocus and go deeper into your breathing. There are two focusing strategies for dealing with pain: You can either go deeper into it, or direct your mind away from it. In both cases breathing is central to the pain management process.

Going Into The Pain:

When you experience pain, you can use it to go deeper into your breathing. Specifically, think of your breathing rhythm. Pain can disorganize that rhythm. It can cause contraction and shorten your breath. What is essential is that you re-establish your rhythm and increase positive energy flow to the affected area. The easiest and most powerful way to do that is with breathing. As you re-strengthen your breathing rhythm, think of creating ease (rather than dis-ease) where the pain is located. Imagine sending and allowing more blood and oxygen to flow into the tense area. If your quads are hurting or cramping, think of releasing tension in those muscles and allow a soothing energy to flow through that area. You can assign a color to that energy depending on what you need: **red** or **gold** for warmth, **blue** or **green** for coolness.

Release the tension, breathe, and send an easing energy (so more oxygen and blood can flow) into and through your pain. If you fight it, you will increase tension and magnify the pain. Remember, whatever we resist, persists. Use the pain for more rhythm or ease. Build up your pain tolerance. It is a measure of mental toughness. Learn and know that you can handle pain better than anybody else.

Ron Hayman, a former world-class cyclist, believed he handled and used pain better than the competition did. If/when he was hurting, Hayman would be smiling and thinking, "Good…cause if it's hurting me, it's killing them." Hayman also shared an idea about how he would approach any race that he had aspirations of winning.

> "I would play every card I had throughout the race to get into a position to win. But in the case that I realized I could

> not win, due to bad legs, superior opponents, or simply being outgunned team-wise, I made damned sure the eventual winner would pay dearly in terms of pain, and would truly deserve the win. That not only ensured that the winner wasn't a fluke, long-shot winner, but it also ensured I was respected, if not feared, in the next race."[62]

Like Ron Hayman, Sean Kelly said,

> "Everybody else is suffering as well, and a good many are probably suffering more. I used to convince myself of that, and it helped.... The ability to suffer is very important—you just can't get results without it. Everybody suffers in cycling, but the great riders can suffer that bit more.... Some people have it naturally, but yes, you can also train yourself to suffer more, and everybody can improve that ability. You train it by pushing the barrier up a little more and more each time over many weeks and months. In the classics, you may be suffering after five hours and still have an hour and a half to go; and in the Grand Tours you have to survive weeks of it. So it helps if you have ways of coping."[63]

Going Away From The Pain:

It is also possible to send your mind away from the pain. Again, you will need to breathe first and rediscover the rhythm you had before the pain set it; then send your thoughts away from the body or body part that hurts. Direct your mind to the road in front of you, to some landmark such as a bridge, or up to and over the top of a hill. If you see people down the road, think of reeling them in. Think of rhythm. Think of lightness. Focus on a power word such as *strength* or *energy*. Contemplate an accomplishment at work. Recall a wonderful holiday you had last year. Use pain as a reminder to breathe and spin the wheel, then refocus on something positive.

Australian Felicity Wardlaw described an interesting dissociation technique that helped her become National Champion.

> "I developed a series of power thoughts, power words, and power images. I imagined I was a panther. I could see myself looking through the eyes of this panther, in that I was fast, relaxed, smooth, powerful, and lean. I practiced this during several training sessions, and during the Nationals I really used this to overcome the pain and transfer it away from my legs."[64]

Caution: Many riders believe that pain is inevitable, i.e., a sign that you are working hard. But the foundation of optimal cycling is not based on self-destruction. You must nurture your experience and judgment in order to gauge when pain is positively telling you that you are pushing yourself enough, or when it is a signal to be heeded with caution.

PEGGY: I started coaching a semi-pro racer after he pushed himself so hard, he passed out and crashed in a criterium. Riders sometimes bonk in training rides, missing the cues that they need more sustenance. These are terribly hard on your body and could be avoided.

CYCLE WISDOM

"I think experience comes into play. It's definitely easy to try and push hard on the pedals for the win, but it's knowing not to exert yourself too much 'cause you know you're going to blow up, and can't sustain that.... So I think that's a big part of it as well, just understanding your body and know how deep you can go."

—Geraint Thomas, Great Britain, 2x Olympic Gold Medalist, Tour de France Winner[65]

HOMEWORK

Right Feeling

Continue to work on creating feelings of ease and power as they relate to riding a bike.

1. 1x 10-minute breathing session every day. Breathe easily and imagine yourself riding your bike with ease, speed, and excellent form.
2. On the bike, think about your breath as a wheel. Work at spinning the wheel and generating power when you experience fatigue, climb, initiate a sprint, and do interval training.
3. Choose three power thoughts or words that you can use when you ride. Rehearse them several times and combine them with your breathing exercises prior to reading the next chapter.

Mastering Pain

Experiment with the two approaches to managing pain:

1. **Going Into The Pain:** Use pain to breathe and spin the wheel. Breathe deeper. Move into your pain. Calm it, open up the tension, and flow with it.
2. **Going Away From The Pain:** Use pain to breathe and spin the wheel. Move away from the pain by focusing your thoughts on a landmark, other riders, feeling light, on a power word, or a pleasant memory.

In this section on Right Feeling, we explored ways of using breathing to shift our feelings. Work with conscious breathing, the release reflex, sending energy out, and blowing off tension to manage challenges and pain more effectively. Practicing these techniques as you train makes you physically and mentally tougher.

RIGHT ATTITUDE

In this section (Chapters 7, 8, and 9), we discuss attitudes of commitment, confidence, as well as pride and love. These elements of character are crucial in nurturing success. Right Attitude is a way of thinking that predisposes one to being more successful. With a Right Attitude, almost anything is possible. Remember, attitude is a matter of choice...and you are the chooser.

CHAPTER 7
Commitment

> **CYCLE WISDOM**
>
> "The best mental attitude wins…mindset is what counts."
>
> *—Julien Jurdie, France, UCI WorldTeam AG2R–Citroën Directeur Sportif*[66]

SAUL: I don't think anything represents attitude more accurately than being a person of character. Character is what enables us to fulfill our potential. Character is the ability to compete and persevere. In my book *Why Teams Win*, I describe nine keys to success. And while cycling is often a non-team sport, these same keys still apply. Commitment, confidence, and identity are three of the keys that promote team success. They will also help you be a successful cyclist.

> **CYCLE WISDOM**
>
> "To be a champion you need first, before anything, the physical capability which comes from birth. Then it's vital to have a strong character or courage. Finally, you must have the ambition to always push yourself."
>
> *—Eddy Merckx, Belgium, Legendary Champion Racer*[67]

Are you really committed? Success begins with motivation. Motivation moves us to action. It's about desire, goals, and commitment. As we said at the outset of the book, goals work. Setting goals clarifies direction and increases success, it's putting things in priority and purpose. But setting goal and repeating your goal statement aren't enough; you have to do the work. Commitment is the willingness to pay the price and do what is necessary to get the result you want.

CYCLE WISDOM

"To win you have to believe you deserve it. During a long, hard race I remind myself of how hard I train, I train to win!"

—Leah Goldstein, Canada, RAAM Winner, Women's and Overall[68]

CYCLE WISDOM

"There were times when I let up too soon, when I could have pushed longer and harder, another 100 meters to catch the break. And when I reflect back on it, I realize I was right there...why didn't I give it everything? It's the would'ves, could'ves, should'ves... we've all experienced."

—Steve Bauer, Canada, Olympic Medalist, UCI ProTeam Israel–Premier Tech Directeur Sportif[69]

CYCLE WISDOM

"The brain is the most powerful muscle in the body. Racing smarts can often provide better results than talent or ability. Of course, a certain talent level is required to put a rider 'in the game.' Cycling luck can also determine the outcome of a race, and good racing often leads to good luck. But above all, determination and a will to overcome (including the deepest suffering that all cyclists experience) is the way champions are made, and what separates winners from losers. This is true for the pros and amateurs as well."

—Sylvan Adams, Canada/Israel, 2x Masters World Champion, UCI ProTeam Israel–Premier Tech Co-Owner[70]

CYCLE WISDOM

"Some people might think it's come easy or quick for me, but I've had a lot of struggles along the way. Nothing ever comes easy. You know, I had to work extremely, extremely hard just to be in good shape for this race [Vuelta]. And just being in good shape doesn't get you far really. You have to know how to ride in the peloton, know how to manage yourself and manage your energy."

—Sepp Kuss, U.S.A., Tour de France Stage, Vuelta a España Stage, Overall GC Winner[71]

Saul: The Japanese have a wonderful expression *kaizen* which means a commitment to continuous improvement.

Your commitment is a reflection of your motivation. If your goal is to reach the top of the mountain, the way up is one step at a time, rain or shine. Taking the time, spending the energy, and making it happen are what commitment is all about. In cycling, one step at a time means doing the day-to-day physical and mental training needed to build up the fitness base, skill sets, productive focus, emotional control, and positive attitude required to excel. It's making yourself more response-able and cycle-tough. Consistent hard work is an expression of commitment, and it is essential to success. Many past cycling greats offer the same advice for riders wanting to excel at the highest level.

PEGGY: For me, nothing illustrates commitment more clearly than athletes who make comebacks from major injuries or illness. Take Georgia Simmerling, the Olympic alpine ski racer who became a Team Pursuiter and an Olympic bronze medalist. She returned to ski cross, had a horrific crash, but is recovering and aiming for the track again. The accounts of her needing help to be clipped into the pedals and doing six hours a day of rehab are astounding examples of her commitment.

Adversity challenges commitment. Here are two of our favorite adversity quotes.

1. "Adversity causes some to break…and others to break records."
2. "Adversity happens for a reason. It can show us how much we want something."

Commitment is the willingness to put in the necessary time and effort to overcome any adversity, and excel. Willingness means making a choice. Choose to shift to Right Focus, Right Feeling, and Right Attitude.

The following statement by NFL Hall of Fame player and coach, Forrest Gregg, really sums it up.

> "To be a winner one must be totally committed.... Total commitment means being willing to do whatever is necessary to become successful. One must be willing to work hard, to push themselves physically until it hurts.... To be a winner one must be willing to make sacrifices.... If you want to be a winner, you will give up anything that does not help you become better at your sport. All athletes are not endowed with the same physical abilities. One can, and many before you have, overcome a lack of ability with extra effort. These people are totally committed."[72]

Or consider this popular sport truism, "Hard work beats talent when talent doesn't work hard."

In everything she has done to date, Leah Goldstein has excelled by combining talent with an incredible work ethic. At the age of 12, she was the Canadian junior taekwondo champion, and won the World Kickboxing Championship at age 17. She then moved to Israel, joined the army, and became a duathlon champion. At 30, Goldstein returned to Canada and became a pro cyclist. It took her half a dozen years to become a world-class racer, and then at 41, she became an ultra-endurance bike racer. In 2011, she won the solo Race Across America (RAAM) for women. Ten years later, in 2021, at the age of 51, Goldstein beat everyone, winning the overall solo RAAM. Her commitment to training is exemplary.

> "When I go into a race, my main objective is to win it. I don't race to finish the race. I race to win. And, I will do everything I can in my preparation and training to make that

> happen. So when I experience the little lows, I think about all the hard work I put into this. I have very high standards for myself and also the way I train. I put everything else on the shelf when I'm training for something specific. I focus on that one thing and having that in my mind is enough to pull me through because in my training, I try to replicate the things I'm going to be going through during the race. That's what we do with our practice races. In training, sometimes I just want to get off the bike for five minutes, but I don't because I know it will take 30 minutes of hard work to get back to where I was. You just have to play these little games with yourself and have enough confidence with how you prepare for this. That's why I say that ultra-endurance racing is probably 30% physical and 70% mental."[73]

Goldstein described training indoors during the Canadian winter for the Race Across America. She was on her trainer pedaling for 10 to 12 hours while looking at a blank wall. In her own words:

> "…because you are replicating race conditions and when racing there are no distractions, no TV, no music…and I did this for 10–12 hours straight, and when I get off the bike to sleep, it's for one or two hours because that's what I'll do when I'm racing. When I taught indoor trainer classes, I never used music because you can't and shouldn't use music on the road. It's dangerous. You have to learn to push yourself without that. You have to learn to do that on your own, with just your heartbeat, your breathing, and the rhythm of your body as your music. No extra stimulation. Don't look at a screen. In racing, all I have to look for hours is the road and my heart rate, so that's how to train, as close as you can to reality. You are going to be staring at the road for hours and hours, and you are going to be uncomfortable… so be uncomfortable when you train. Then there's no

surprises. Then the thinking becomes, yeah, I've done this in training so I can do this. Not only do I not have TV, music, or a phone, I train with the lights off. Light helps you to stay awake, so training without light makes the training that much more difficult. In the follow vehicle, we have changed the lights which are brighter, and that helps me to stay awake, but I didn't do that in my training; when it got dark, it got dark. All I had was a little flashlight I could turn on to see if I was on pace. Some people say they can't ride without their music, well then you are not racing or training, you are just going for a leisurely ride…and that's not how you train. Racing with music is not allowed, and riding with music is a recipe for disaster. If you must do it, do it indoors."[74]

CYCLE WISDOM

"Want to improve...to be the best you can be? Push yourself: you can't get good by staying home. If you want to get, fast you have to go where the 'fast guys' are."

—Steve Larsen, U.S.A., National Team Road Racer [75]

One of the fast guys is 4x Tour de France champion Chris Froome. Reporting on an intense altitude training block and putting on some big miles in preparation for the coming season, Froome chuckled.

"There's not really much to do up here other than ride your bike. Strength sessions in the morning off the bike—then on the bike during the day—get back—have a meal—have a massage—then go to bed—and then repeat. It's pretty much the life of a pro cyclist. It's pretty boring."[76]

Using It

Commitment means using it. We mentioned this earlier in the book, and it's worth repeating. If your goal is to be the best cyclist you can be…then whatever comes up, you have to use it. If you don't use it…it can use you. So learn how to use it, whatever the situation, challenge, or obstacle. If you have a good ride, use it to reaffirm your ability and build your confidence. If you have a poor ride, use it to improve your training process and refocus on the positive. The process of using it is pretty straightforward. It involves changing programs (as described in Chapter 5), clearing the screen on your mental computer, and refocusing on the positive. When people perceive a challenging stimulus, their initial response is often automatic. Using it is about activating the release reflex: releasing tension, negativity, or anxiety, breathing in energy and power, and refocusing on the positive—on what you want to do on the road, track, or hill, on being a star, being a winner…on being a tiger.

Justin Williams, founder of the L39ION Team, used his discomfort with the U.S.A. racing scene to motivate him to create a team opportunity for Black and Latino racers. He said being a lone Black racer, unable to score a pro contract "broke him." But he "used it" to propel him to help others not go through the same situation.[77]

Mental toughness is the ability to *use it* under pressure. Winners are not free from disappointment, fear, and negativity. Like everyone else, they experience uncertainty and doubt. They just don't dwell on it. Instead, they use it to refocus and stay on the power channel. Winners use everything.

CYCLE WISDOM

"I've learned that I have to accept that even if I'm World Champion, I can't win every race I want and when I do lose, I have to learn from that for the future."

—Julian Alaphilippe, France, 2x Pro Road World Champion[78]

One school of thought is that if you want to improve at something, anything, get involved with people (athletes) who are more successful than you. Then you will get better. Observing their focus, determination, work ethic, and ability to use it, can provide inspiring and positive modeling. Set a standard of commitment for yourself and model it for your teammates. Become more aware of what is happening around you, and whatever presents itself, choose to use it.

PEGGY: When an athlete feels badly about a performance–they missed a winning move, they crashed, they went off course–that's the time to refocus. To use it. Go back and review, find where the mistake was made and how to perform differently in the future. After a teammate missed the podium in the Commonwealth Games, it took some time before she was ready to review the race footage. When she was ready, we sat together and watched the final sprint unfold. She was able to see that she let it come down to a bunch sprint which reduced her opportunities, and that she did not initiate the final sprint which weakened her chances. She was able to use that information to change her tactics, and then ride solo to win or jump first to beat the bunch.

CYCLE WISDOM

"The road to success is like ups and downs all the time. Maybe in the end, you are in the top. But there's a long way to success. You have to pick yourself up after those disappointments and just find the motivation again."

—Wout van Aert, Belgium, 3x World Cyclocross Champion, World Road Championship Medalist[79]

Wout van Aert on the cobbles in the yellow jersey, Tour de France.

CYCLE WISDOM

"Of course, I have some regrets and of course, I think I could have done some things differently, but I try not to look back so much. I try to learn from my mistakes, and I try to learn what I can do better next year, so I can change second and third places for victories."

—Jakob Fuglsang, Denmark, Olympic Road Race Medalist[80]

Here are suggestions for how to *use it* in different situations.

- When you have a good ride: Take a breath, acknowledge yourself, think, *that's who I am* or *the tiger is hunting*. Take another breath (or two), and get ready to hunt again.
- When you have a poor ride: Take a breath, think, *that's not me*, see yourself making adjustments and riding great. Then take a breath (or two), and get ready to hunt again.
- When an opponent is barking at you: Take a breath, keep hunting, spin the wheel, and push forward.
- When coaches are criticizing you: Take a breath, hear what is being said, acknowledge you are a good rider, and work hard in practice on what will make you better.
- When a teammate does something exceptional: Be positive, acknowledge it, take a breath, match his/her effort on your next ride.

SAUL: It was the North American Cycling Championship in Indianapolis. I had been counseling with Curt, a powerful young track cyclist, the best in Canada and one of the best in the world. We were sitting at the velodrome, talking and waiting for his race: the kilo. The kilo is a race against the clock, three laps around the 333-meter track, at maximum speed. As we waited, we could see dark gray clouds forming in the distance...and getting closer. Curt started to get nervous. He was ready to race…and if it rained, the track would get wet and the race might be delayed. I was attempting to be calm, positive, and reassuring, with the occasional, *it'll be fine*. Then it happened. As we sat talking, a bird flew over and shat on one of Curt's massive thighs. I remember him looking down, then looking up, and saying with a somewhat perplexed and anxious voice, "A bird just shat on my leg." To which I replied, "That's a really positive omen. If a bird shits on your head, it's a world record. If it shits on your leg, it's a track record." Curt laughed. His mood changed. We waited a little longer. The rains held off. And then Curt raced and won…setting a new track record.

When shit happens, USE IT!

SAUL: I frequently speak to management and coaching groups, and sport teams on winning, teamwork, and leadership. I routinely ask the groups to rank five key qualities in terms of their relationship to team success. The five qualities are talent, leadership, strategy, commitment, and chemistry. Over the years, almost every group has rated commitment as the most important.

Three additional qualities and expressions of commitment are perseverance, resilience, and discipline.

Perseverance

Perseverance is the quality of a winner. According to 30th president of the U.S.A., Calvin Coolidge,

> "Nothing in this world can take the place of persistence. Talent will not; nothing is more common than unsuccessful men with talent. Genius will not; unrewarded genius is almost a proverb. Education will not; the world is full of educated derelicts. Persistence and determination are omnipotent. The slogan *press on* has solved and always will solve the problems of the human race."[81]

Saul asked Benjamin Perry, a pro Tour racer, what he believed to be the most important mental quality to be a successful world-class cyclist.

> "For me, perseverance is definitely number one. In anyone's story, even Chris Froome's, there are always moments when you're not the best…when you are struggling. You just have to keep fighting, because there's always challenges. Maybe you're strong but there are riders with more experience than you. And in road racing, it doesn't always translate that you can suffer more to get a better result. No, you have to learn to play the game. For road racing particularly, perseverance is number one. You have to learn to do the hard yards. When young riders ask me what it takes to make it and what to do, I say if you really want to be a pro, go to Belgium, France, or Spain, where there are lots of people racing, and where the roads are narrow and you really have to fight and battle to compete and to try to win."[82]

Pro cyclists understand that commitment and mental toughness are required to win.

CYCLE WISDOM

"LeMond was in trouble. He had a bout of diarrhea. He rode by me with 30 km to go, surrounded by his domestiques, bringing him to the front. God, the smell was terrible. It was rolling down his leg. I know if it was me, I would stop. But then, I'm not capable of winning the Tour de France. He is, and I suppose that's the difference."

—Paul Kimmage, Ireland, Former Pro Racer, Journalist, commenting on Greg LeMond in the Tour de France[83]

CYCLE WISDOM

"Cycling takes so many hours to train and so many years to be really strong. Being good at cycling doesn't happen because you train hard one year."

—*Rune Hoydahl, Norway, Mountain Bike World Cup Champion in Downhill and Cross-Country*[84]

CYCLE WISDOM

"You have to be hungry, have an edge. That's what matters. You may not be the best, but with determination and drive, you can beat anyone."

—*Mark Madiot, France, 2x Paris–Roubaix Winner, UCI WorldTeam Groupama–FDJ Directeur Sportif*[85]

There are many excellent examples in sport of athletes who were told they did not have the right stuff, or individuals who overcame serious illness and injury, and despite the odds, persisted and ultimately achieved at the highest level. Here are two examples.

PEGGY: When I think of perseverance, one rider that really stands out for me is Marion Clignet of France. But Clignet didn't always race for France. We were U.S. National teammates before the U.S. team made a decision to stop supporting Clignet because she is epileptic. Clignet discovered her passion for cycling when she lost her diver's license for a year due to her first seizure, at age 22. Her bicycle became an excellent replacement for her car, allowing her to get to work and giving her a sense of freedom and independence. As she rode back and forth, she kept wanting to break her records. Eventually, she tried a race and loved the adrenaline and excitement. It then became her dream to make it to the very top of her sport, to race with the best and win.

MARION CLIGNET: I won the U.S. National Road Championships in 1990, at age 27. I wasn't allowed to compete for the U.S.A. in the World Championships because the U.S. Cycling Federation decided that having epilepsy made me a risk to the team. That was very painful. I never felt welcome there or supported, save for a few people.[86]

PEGGY: Clignet is a dual citizen; her parents are French. After Team U.S.A.'s decision, she was invited to join the French cycling team. This was before the UCI ruled that license holders could not change countries after being licensed in a previous country.

MARION CLIGNET: Some French cyclists told me to come over to France, I went in August and [finished] the season there. I was really upset by not being accepted for the U.S. team, but having something else to focus on really motivated me. Epilepsy really is responsible for my success, because it always made me push myself harder. I don't think I would have made it to where I am now if it wasn't for having epilepsy, as it always made me push myself harder.

PEGGY: Clignet felt she had to prove herself better, deserving of a spot on teams regardless of this taboo. Working with her neurologist, she was able to find medication that controlled her epilepsy. However, she struggled to find the right balance, experiencing fluctuations with her weight and energy levels. She received a lot of comments about her weight, adding diet and food concerns to her troubles.

MARION CLIGNET: When you are thin, they say how fit and fabulous you look, when you are heavy, they say you look horrible. Europeans can be harsh about that.

PEGGY: Politics also presented some challenges. At that time, another French racer had a stranglehold on the women's racing scene. That rider's negative, hyper-critical attitude reduced enthusiasm and opportunity for women's racing. Then the French Federation refused to allow Clignet to use the Graeme Obree's "superman position" on the track, reducing her chances of winning the pursuit at the Atlanta Olympics.

MARION CLIGNET: I knew I was racing for 2nd. It was difficult. My main competitor in Atlanta, Antonella Bellutti [Italy], was using it, and I let that get in my head–she beat me. I managed to avenge myself and win the World Championships while breaking the world record a few weeks later [while using the "superman position"]. 80% of sport is mental.[87]

PEGGY: Clignet has a three-year gap in her resume. After the 1996 Olympics, she began to experience pain and arthritis in her knees and feet. She was diagnosed with a genetic disorder…another hurdle. She was also working full-time, trying to maintain fitness by swimming ("I swim like a dead cow"[88]), and continuously assuring the French Federation that she would return. Three years later, she did return–winning double gold on the track World Championships. Despite all these challenges, Clignet has had a remarkable cycling career, winning over a dozen national titles, World Championships, and Olympic medals. That's perseverance.

MARION CLIGNET: You're always your own support. Indeed, sometimes you are the only one who believes.[89]

Clignet continues advocating for epilepsy with a fundraising charity ride and by organizing a pro women's Tour in the Pyrenees.

SAUL: Barry "Baz" Lycett grew up in Yorkshire, started cycling when he was 14 years old, and immediately fell in love with the sport. Upon completing high school, like all young men in his town, Baz was directed to the coal mines. However, after a short stint underground, Baz realized that being an underground miner would affect his breathing and impair his cycling, so he quit and found other work to support his passion. He was part of the local club, riding and racing whenever he could. Carless, he often rode his bike to race venues, carrying his racing wheels with him. As his prowess developed, Baz focused on winning a National Championship…and after 10 years of racing, he won the British Grass Track Championship over five miles. Grass track racing lent itself to three of Baz's attributes: it helped if you were short, smart, and determined. Baz was all three. Baz set his next goal to represent his country. It took him another three years to achieve it, representing England in grass track racing in the British West Indies, racing on grass cricket grounds in Barbados, Trinidad, and Guyana. Baz moved to Canada in 1969, and started the Anglia Cycling Club in Vancouver with three other British riders. Being the most experienced of the group and always willing to contribute, he also began coaching. In 1972, one of Baz's cycling students competed for Canada in the Olympics. His coaching abilities and reputation grew, and eventually he became Canada's national cycling coach. Many of Canada's cyclists who went on to World Championships, Olympics, and pro racing were riders he coached. The list includes Ron Hayman, Pierre Harvey, Jocelyn Lovell, Hugh Walton, Adrian Prosser, Steve Bauer, Karen Strong, Alison Sydor, Curt Harnett, and Alex Stieda–an Olympian and the first Canadian to wear the yellow jersey in the Tour de France.

ALEX STIEDA: We learned everything we needed to know about road and track racing from Baz. including race tactics, gear selection, training, intervals, heat zones, recovery, nutrition, even the secrets of choosing the right tubular glue! I have incredible memories of going to Nationals with the B.C. team and winning every event that we entered, all due to Baz's oversight and attention to detail.[90]

SAUL: Baz coached for several decades. In the early 1970s, coaching at the provincial and national levels was on a volunteer basis. Therefore, he worked in the winter (October–March) then quit the job in order to be available for full-time, volunteer coaching. Those winter jobs included working in a copper mine, a meat-packing plant, and a beer-bottling plant.

BARRY "BAZ" LYCETT: These kinds of jobs never got me down. I knew there was an end date…and then I was back to cycling.

SAUL: He later spent a number of winters in Europe assisting professional riders at dozens of six-day track races.

BARRY "BAZ" LYCETT: Looking back on those days, when I was traveling on a shoestring in countries where I did not speak the language was challenging. But none of this was a "sacrifice"–I did it with the end goal in mind of becoming a better coach.

SAUL: Baz's passion for cycling has never abated. Now in his eighties, he still rides three times a week, year-round. As a matter of fact, the day I spoke with him, he was preparing for a 100K ride, Ryder Hesjedal's Tour of Victoria the following day. Baz has been riding and racing for almost 70 years. I asked him what has kept the cycling passion alive.

BARRY "BAZ" LYCETT: I didn't ride for my health. I rode because it was fun… and it still is fun. Whenever you have a bad day, just go for a ride. In my life, I followed my front wheel…and I loved doing it.[91]

Baz is the personification of passion and persistence. Winning athletes and winning teams are positive. They believe in themselves. They believe in the goal they are working toward and in their process that will get them there. That belief stimulates them to act and persevere.

Barry Lycett coaching B.C. Senior Pursuit Team, National Championships.

SAUL: I experienced the benefits of persistence early in my forty-plus years' career. I recall telephoning the head coach of an NHL team and leaving several messages with his secretary. When he didn't return my call, I tried again, again, again, and again. I must have called and left half a dozen messages, but still, there was no return call. Then, on my seventh call, he picked up the phone. "It's Dr. Saul Miller speaking." His response was somewhat sarcastic, "Well, you certainly are persistent." I replied, "Persistence is the quality of a winner. You expect your players to persist in the game, don't you?" His mood shifted, he laughed. "Yes, I do. What can I do for you?" I explained I wanted an opportunity to meet with him to talk about what I could do to help the team be more successful. Somewhat unenthusiastically, he agreed to an appointment. We met in his office several days later and shortly thereafter, he referred several players to me. When I began consulting with the players it was midseason and they had won only three of their previous 21 games. The team's performance improved dramatically, and they made it into the playoffs, kept winning, and went all the way to the Stanley Cup finals. What is especially interesting about this story is how my comment, "Persistence is the quality of a winner," appeared to open a door to our meeting. It literally changed his thinking from *this guy is a nuisance* to *this person is determined*. My perseverance came from a sincere belief that I had something useful to contribute and a commitment to make a positive difference. The coach sensed my determination, and an opportunity was presented. The results suggest my involvement did contribute to a significant improvement in performance.

Resilience

Resilience is a subset of perseverance. It is the capacity to spring back from difficulties. Cyclists who aspire to excellence inevitably experience difficulties, challenges, and injuries. Their ability to bounce back and persevere is a measure of their passion, determination, and mental toughness.

Maggie Coles-Lyster's blog post on redefining resilience is an excellent illustration of commitment in an internationally competitive and mentally tough cyclist.

> "The bell was ringing as we flew into the last lap of the track race, shoulder to shoulder, trying to get an edge over the other riders…well, actually, I don't remember anything about that race.
>
> My first clear memory was waking up, lying trackside, surrounded by paramedics holding white sheets draped around me to keep spectator eyes away. Our team therapist was crouched behind me, supporting my head. The confusion I felt in that moment was overpowering, as I watched riders ride around me, waiting to exit the track. I couldn't understand why I was lying on the ground and was not out there with them. It just made no sense at all. There

was no pain, everything just moved in slow motion. I felt like I was inside a fish bowl, observing life take place on the outside. 'What happened?' I remember asking my therapist.

'You crashed.'

I was in and out of consciousness until getting to the hospital, where the pain meds must have kicked in and the memories turned from confusion to hilarity. I remember waking up to a very attractive doctor standing over me with a pair of scissors. It took less than a minute for me to realize that he was about to cut me out of my cycling kit. I was highly embarrassed but also felt ridiculously giggly under the impartial gazes of the rest of the medical staff in the room.

Afterwards a nurse came to clean up the bloody mess that was my face. She noticed that my nose ring had completely disappeared into my nose, and set out to remove it. No way was I going to let her take it out for that meant the hole would close up and I would have to get it re-pierced. I put up a fuss until she reluctantly put my piercing back in place. The real MVP of the hospital, in my opinion, was that nurse, and I felt comically triumphant in my success of saving my nose ring.

The CAT scan revealed that I had four fractures in my cheek, a couple of broken ribs, a punctured lung, and lots of pooled blood in my face, along with a severe concussion.

Remarkably, I only spent one night in the hospital, before being cleared to head back to the Airbnb with my dad who, luckily, was over there with me. I couldn't fly home due to my punctured lung, for risk that it would collapse, so we spent two weeks in Copenhagen, which sounds great if I wasn't spending the majority of the time sleeping over 16 hours a night, frequently visiting various doctors, and consuming five different painkillers a day.

On my 19th birthday, I was cleared to fly home. Not exactly how I had imagined celebrating it.

Once home and clear of a concussion, I was on the hunt to get back on the bike as quickly as possible. I thought this was what being resilient was. And remarkably, it worked. Or I thought it worked for me, as three weeks later, I was in the full swing of training again and prepping for the road season ahead.

Just as I felt I was getting back to the place I was before the crash, I hit the pavement again.

This time I was taken out by another rider while pre-riding a road race course. Another brief loss of consciousness, another concussion, and a ride in the back of a cop car to get me home. The hardest part was that I still had to start the race so that the team could race, with the agreement that I would pull out after 1 km. Absolute. Torture. It was the first race I pulled myself out of, and was definitely the right call as you should never race concussed, but that was a huge test of my willpower. And once again, it was back on the now familiar road to recovery.

Again, I tried to flex my resilience and be back in the peloton as soon as my concussion was clear.

This time I slowly became aware that something just wasn't right. I would end up at the back of the pack of riders without knowing how I got there. I would 'check out' of sprints if I felt they were getting dangerous. I knew what I had to do in a race but couldn't control these unconscious reactions that were, ironically, putting me in more dangerous positions than I was in.

I blamed my weight, form, and fitness for why I felt like I sucked at bike racing and would finish the races in tears. I started becoming self-conscious in these areas, which was doing me no favors on top of what I was going through.

> Trauma is defined as 'a deeply disturbing or distressing experience' and 'physical injury.' The latter is easily recognizable and treatable, however, we often overlook or push aside the psychological trauma that can severely impact our life after an incident. I was a victim of overlooking the trauma, too. I didn't remember the first crash, or the pain, or even the race. I figured as soon as my wounds healed, I would be okay.
>
> It wasn't until later that year, that I realized I wouldn't be winning another bike race until I addressed my still gaping, psychological wounds.
>
> What has helped me recover psychologically and get me back to a place where I can be on top of my game in a race are some of the same techniques described earlier in this book: conscious breathing and meditation, positive self-talk (looking in the mirror daily and acknowledging my strengths as a rider), positive high-performance visualization and awakening the jaguar (powerful animal image). Also, my determination not just to get back to my previous competitive level but to push myself to be the very best that I can be in a race, in my day-to-day training, and in my life."[92]

Coles-Lyster is back racing in top form and is training for the next Olympics. Maggie's grit and determination, while exemplary, are representative of the heroes of the sport. Greg LeMond and Fabio Jakobsen came back from near death experiences to win at the Tour de France. Chloe Dygert, a multiple World Champion, crashed then came back from leg surgery, Epstein-Barr virus, and heart surgery, to win two more World Championships, similar to Marion Clignet's three-year gap before returning to win another two world titles. And Leah Goldstein, RAAM winner, had to have her braids tied to the back of her sport bra and heart monitor strap to keep her head up so she could complete the 4,800 km Race Across America.

SAUL: In four decades consulting with some of the world's best athletes in over 35 different sports, there is no sport where athletes have demonstrated more determination, grit, pain tolerance, and talent than in elite bike racing.

Discipline

Discipline is another characteristic of commitment and winning. Legendary basketball coach Bobby Knight saw discipline and commitment as one.

> "It has always been my thought that the most important single ingredient in success in athletics and in life is discipline. I have many times felt that this word is the most ill-defined in our language. My definition of discipline is: Do what has to be done, when it has to be done, as well as it can be done. And, do it that way all the time."[93]

CYCLE WISDOM

"When I say rest, I don't mean lying on the beach, drinking beer. Rest is rest from the bike, not rest from training."

—Edward "Eddie B" Borysewicz, Poland, Team U.S.A. National Coach[94]

To achieve success one has to maintain a focus on what is relevant and tune out all those stimuli— however appealing and alluring— that could be seen as distracting or irrelevant. To succeed one has to maintain a disciplined, winning mindset.

CYCLE WISDOM

"Do not give up when you find out that you have to suffer greatly to get results. Never forget that winners are the ones who can suffer the best. It's the no-hopers who cannot suffer. The inability to suffer is almost always the real reason riders do not succeed in our sport. The person who can suffer the best has the best chance of getting to the top."

—Charles Ruys, The Netherlands, Cycling Coach and Manager, 6 Day Race Organizer[95]

CYCLE WISDOM

"Five hundred meters from the finish line. You get an adrenaline rush. You know the race is in play. You know you can lose everything at that moment. So you are totally focused."

—David Gaudu, France, La Vuelta a España and Critérium du Dauphiné Stage Winner, 4th Overall in Tour De France[96]

Larson Craddock provides another excellent example of a disciplined pro racer who turned pain and disappointment into a *use it* experience, in a couple different ways. Craddock was asked which pain was worse, fracturing his scapula in the first stage of the 2018 Tour de France or being left off the 2019 EF Tour de France team.

> "Tough question. They're very different kinds of pain. The injury in 2018 was just massive discomfort on the bike…

> but I was there. I came to the Tour ready to race. I put so much work in. My wife made a ton of sacrifices to support me every step of the way, and I just couldn't stop racing. [Riding with a fractured scapula and other assorted injuries, Craddock finished all 21 stages of the Tour and raised almost $20,000 to rebuild a velodrome in Houston, Texas, that had been damaged by Hurricane Harvey]. While it was very tough, I wouldn't say it was painful, it was mostly discomfort that I felt. Not being selected to the Tour team definitely hurt…like a stab to the heart. You make the same sacrifices. Not just me but my wife and daughter all doing their best to support me every step of the way. You have the conversation where you are told you are not racing in the Tour de France, my first thought is I've let my loved ones down, and I didn't accomplish the goal that we all set out to do. That was tough, tough to swallow for a bit of time. At some point, you've got to move on. You've got to focus on the positive of the situation. I was able to spend that summer with my family, being back home in Texas, enjoying it there and just taking that as a bit of motivation forward. In the end, when I look back on it, I had what was a great end of the season with the Vuelta and the World Championships. And for me that opportunity wouldn't have been there, if I had been at the Tour last year."

When asked how is he better now because of that disappointment, Craddock answered,

> "You go through these lows and down points. Everyone does it. All of our lives are like roller coasters. One thing I realized, and I actually realized this during the 2018 Tour, it's kind of what you make out of them. And that year in the Tour, when I raced with a fractured scapula, it pointed out to me that things usually don't go exactly as you planned them. That doesn't mean it's a failure. That doesn't mean

that you've done everything wrong. What matters from then on out is how you react to that, and how you move forward. And one thing you learn in the down moments is success isn't always what you set out for it to be, but it doesn't mean you can't be successful."[97]

CYCLE WISDOM

"My biggest fear isn't crashing the bike at 85 mph and losing skin. It's sitting in my chair at 90 and thinking, 'I wish I'd done more.'"

—*Graeme Obree, Scotland, Pursuit World Champion*[98]

HOMEWORK

Define Your Commitment

1. Review your SMART cycling goals.
   - What are your long- and short-term goals, both for you individually and for your team?
   - What's your commitment?
   - What price are you willing to pay to achieve your goals?
2. Think of a couple of examples of how you used a cycling situation to take a step(s) closer to your goal.
3. Now identify one thing about your riding that has been using you and getting you down and think of how you can use it to be a

more effective cyclist. See yourself working towards your goals and around those obstacles, shifting from doubts to affirmations.

In Chapter 7, we introduced commitment as one of components of Right Attitude. Commitment is about one's willingness to do whatever is necessary to achieve one's goals. As such, it encompasses goal-directed effort, perseverance, resilience, and learning to use adversity to make you stronger. Commitment builds confidence. We explore confidence in Chapter 8.

CHAPTER 8
Confidence

Confidence is another key to a winning attitude, and it is a significant factor in how one performs. A person who is confident believes he or she can do the job. That belief makes it more likely the job will get done. Two important questions for most athletes are: How do I increase my confidence? How do I transform doubt and negativity into a more positive, confident sense of being a winner? The two most basic ways to build confidence are through success and preparation.

CYCLE WISDOM

"You have to maintain a certain posture as a sprinter. To have a place at the head of affairs where it is really dicey, I have to exude a confidence and strength so people won't mess with me."

—Davis Phinney, U.S.A., Olympic Medalist, Won 320 Races[99]

CYCLE WISDOM

"If you can go further in terms of suffering and sacrifice, then you may have a chance. And that gives you confidence, strength, and a certain serenity about oneself."

—Marc Madiot, France, UCI World Team Groupama–FDJ General Manager[100]

In this chapter, we present a few examples from other sports to illustrate how confidence can directly enhance performance. Relate these examples to your cycling experience.

Success

Success builds confidence.

SAUL: Late one evening, I got a phone call from an NHL coach who was on board the team plane, heading home after a disappointing loss. The team had been losing repeatedly, and this particular defeat was just too much. The coach wanted me to speak to his players the next day about confidence. When I entered the room, the players were all assembled. After being introduced, I asked the group, "What builds confidence?" The room was silent. Finally, the captain said, "Winning…success." Of course, he was right. Success, in the form of winning and performing well, builds confidence. And confidence leads to more success. However, confidence is fragile. If you are a scorer in that sport and you haven't been scoring, anxiety and self-doubt can creep into your thinking. Success erases the self-doubt. It's the same in racing. If you are a talented cyclist with a history of success and the results in your last few races have been disappointing, you may begin to experience anxiety and self-doubt…or maybe, like Chloe Dygert, you won't.

CYCLE WISDOM

"I go into every race thinking I'm going to win."

—Chloe Dygert, U.S.A., 8x Track and Road World Champion, Olympic Medalist[101]

Chloe Dygert, World Championship Time Trial.

SAUL: Dygert's comment speaks to her confidence, demonstrating she is never satisfied or happy. She thinks she can be the best and ride the perfect race. Even when she wins the race, she knows she can be even better.

After winning a time trial, World Champion, Dygert, interviewed with John Croom.

> *Dygert:* "You know I watched the clips. I've seen a replay of it, and there's a few lines I took that were wrong. Obviously, in the moment, it was as hard as I could go, but looking back, thinking back, it was like, what if I could have gone a little harder on the climbs…what if I…"
>
> *Croom:* "You won the World Championship by 1 minute and 40 seconds."
>
> *Dygert:* "I don't care. I'm so annoyed." Dygert added that she had the 3rd fastest overall split (men and women) half way and the 11th fastest split of the men at the end, and that she was greatly displeased with the drop off. "And in the World Juniors, I won that race [TT] by over a minute too, and there were two times I specifically remember zoning out…and I'm still pissed about it, thinking back now. It still frustrates me to no end. There's not one race I'm satisfied with."
>
> *Croom:* "It's wild to think that is frustrating to you. You won a world title, and all you can think about is the few mistakes you made. Speaking of the World Championships, and you've won many, what's probably your most favorite memory of the World Championships? What's your favorite World Championship that you've ever won—road or track?"
>
> *Dygert:* "It's tough to say, and it sounds really shitty to say it like this. My first year racing I won Worlds. So it's such an expectation for me to win now, that if I don't win… it's not the pressure…. It's not that I care about what people think, it's more like why didn't I win?"[102]

PEGGY: It took me more than one season to stop always playing domestique, automatically blocking for teammates in breaks when I was right there when the break formed and could have been in it too. It started to change when I began to say to myself, over and over, *I deserve to be in the break*. I visualized being right in there when breaks formed and saw myself pulling through. Then, gradually, it began to happen: I began to feel more confident, and when I recognized a break was forming, instead of backing off, I pulled through. My race results improved dramatically. Another expression of confidence is feeling accepted and having a sense of belonging with the best riders. Some people take that position quickly; others work their way into it. Talking with racers, one prevalent trait is that women tend to feel they have to work hard enough to earn a position in the break or on the podium. Men don't seem to heed the ranking order as much. They are more comfortable sitting on and taking a sprint win, regardless of their level of experience or how much they contributed to the race.

Strengthening Confidence

SAUL: After an excellent start to the season, Susan, an effective competitive cyclist, lost the edge and her confidence. One day, she called. "Something's off. I'm struggling. In the last three or four races, I wasn't sharp, I'm not making the right reads, I'm missing breaks, and I don't seem to have the jump to get back into the mix. Saul, I don't feel right, and frankly, my confidence is gone." She asked if I could help her regain her confidence and her mojo. "Susan, you are a very capable competitive racer. Top athletes sometimes have periods when they are less effective. If you're worried about it, I'll recommend four things you can do to start winning again."

- First is to remember to relax and breathe.
- Second is positive self-talk. And it's important to know this in your bones and to say it to yourself again and again, that you are a very good cyclist. You are good at every aspect of racing. You know your strengths. You read

races well. You are strong, fit, and fast. You handle the bike well. You are mentally tough. And you love to win. That's who you are. You love to work hard. You love to race. And you win.

- Third is mental rehearsal. As I've said repeatedly, it's helpful to visualize those things you do when you are racing at your best. I suggested you imagine riding the great race. Imagine yourself feeling strong, confident, riding from the front, spinning a big gear, riding with a smile on your face. You are working hard. There are a few good wheels, and you know where they are. Imagine yourself standing up to climb aggressively. Imagine yourself descending smoothly and with speed. Imagine yourself pushing to set up the sprint…you're feeling some pain…but it just makes you tougher, faster. You know you are in the hunt, and you can win…and you are loving the challenge. I want you to run through a scenario like this twice a day, every day. Remember, every time you have a negative or worrisome thought, drop it, breathe in some energy, and turn the wheel.
- Fourth, to sharpen the edge, is to practice on the bike. Practice spinning, powering, climbing, cornering, descending, and sprinting. Practice does make perfect. Follow this advice, and you will be back on the podium.

When I spoke to Susan two weeks later, her mojo and smile had returned, and she was standing on the podium.

EXERCISE 8.1

Strengthening Confidence

Imagine experiencing a challenging time in your career. And then, just as Susan was instructed in Saul's account, use the four tools outlined to turn things around.

1. Relax and breathe—always a good start.
2. Do some mental rehearsal and positive high-performance imagery. Imagine yourself racing at your best.
3. Practice riding strong and smart.
4. Use positive self-talk to repeatedly remind yourself of your strengths as a cyclist.

Here is an example of an innovative confidence boost.

PEGGY: A pro team soigneur related in confidence that occasionally when a racer was struggling and feeling desperate enough, they might reach out to the staff and inquire about the prospect of the staff providing them with some "performance enhancement." The soigneur described how on several occasions the alerted and enlightened staff came up with a creative solution. They placed placebos in specially marked bottles and feeds, pretending it was the "enhancement stuff" the rider had been looking for. In reality, it was just an elaborate deception pulled off by the concerned support staff in pre- and post-race care to give the rider a temporary confidence boost. After the event, they would explain to the racer exactly what had been done, and how the racer had actually performed just fine under their own power. One racer was awed when informed he had won a classic without the "help" he thought he needed. His imagination was the confidence booster that fueled the winning performance. And his newly discovered understanding of what he was capable of doing on his own was a genuine confidence booster for the future.

The number one answer to the question of what builds confidence is success. Success—like riding well—with power, speed, and smarts, outperforming the opposition and winning—builds confidence. But what if you haven't had success lately? What can you do to grow your confidence when you haven't been riding at your best? The answer lies in preparation.

Preparation

Preparation is the second key to building confidence. In discussing the importance of preparation, frequently refer to a high mountain peak seen from the valley below. At first, the task of climbing to the top seems overwhelming. You may lack the confidence and belief that you can do it. However, the task becomes less daunting if you break down the climb into steps and stages, with many steps constituting a stage. If you know from your training that you can take these steps and complete each stage, your confidence that you can complete the climb will grow. In climbing your cycling mountain, visualize yourself taking the steps necessary to build your strength, skills, fitness, and ability to read the competition and the race. Approach your development in steps and stages. Work your SMART goals. Break down the challenge into what is manageable, and do what is necessary.

CYCLE WISDOM

"I used to be so nervous on the start line...and afraid of losing. So I practiced all the moves in sprinting, mastering it all so that when the official's whistle blew, indicating the two sprinters to begin their first lap, I would feel prepared and totally present and my mind would begin calculating every half pedal stroke in order to win. Being prepared quieted my nervousness and enabled me to shift my mind into a winning mode."

—Nelson Vails, U.S.A., Olympic and World Championships Medalist[103]

Regaining confidence and returning to top form following an injury requires the same approach. Set your end goal and some attainable intermediate goals. See yourself doing the basics and performing well at each stage. As you do, your belief in your ability will grow. You will know that you can do it.

SAUL: Just as I advised Susan, use mental rehearsal to visualize yourself doing it, then actually perform it in practice. Finally, make or allow it to happen in race situations. Following are two relevant affirmations worth repeating:

- My mind is a force I use to make things happen
- Self-love is allowing myself to be great.

PEGGY: I asked a group of athletes, "What is the purpose and value of your training? What does it mean that you can do seven hill repeats or nine one-kilometer intervals?" Judging by their blank looks, they hadn't formed a clear connection between the physical training done in workouts, with confidence gained for an upcoming event. What is missing is understanding the specific elements that each event demands, doing that work, and then growing in confidence, knowing that, *I'm prepared*, and therefore, *I can*. A friend placed first in a criterium and afterward said that in training, she had been doing one-kilometer intervals for her track events. She told herself that if she could do that, she could go hard off the front for one kilometer, the distance of the the final lap of this criterium. She led the whole way and won, based on that confidence. A Masters client wrote in his training diary that he didn't feel well but went out and had a really good, hard, group training ride. Now he is confident that he doesn't have to feel great to perform well.

SAUL: My advice, do not just train to train…train to excel.

Separation By Preparation

After winning the Super Bowl, Russell Wilson, the quarterback of the Seattle Seahawks, related that separation is in the preparation was one of the team's guiding principles. "It is the way we prepare that separates us from others."[104]

It is a brilliant principle because it works both up and down. That is, you can separate yourself upward from others by dedicating yourself to a level of physical, skill, and mental preparation, or you can separate yourself downward from others by preparing poorly. Most experienced riders know cyclists who have separated themselves up with their preparation and effort, as well as those cyclists who have separated themselves down with poor preparation.

Clara Honsinger was prepared for the Cyclocross National Championships. It was a goal she had been committed to for some time, and her preparation was rigorous. Everything was set. The body, the mind, the bikes.... Before the start of the race, she got word that the team van carrying her bike had a flat tire. However, Honsinger was able to remain calm about the van flatting out and not having her race bike on time on race day because she was prepared for any and every eventuality. "I definitely did my homework... mentally as well as physically, and that gave me the confidence to know I could handle this glitch and perform well."[105] And perform well she did, winning the Cyclocross National Championship.

SAUL: I frequently tell sport audiences about two football Hall of Famers who highlight the importance of preparation for building confidence. For Bill Parcells, a successful NFL coach who transformed four losing teams (the New York Jets and Giants, New England Patriots, and Dallas Cowboys) into winners, "Preparedness is the key to success. The more you prepare beforehand, the more relaxed and effective you'll be when it counts."[106] Roger Staubach, an All-

Pro NFL quarterback, said about confidence and success, "The most important thing is preparation. You have to do everything you can to be successful. As an athlete I worked really hard to be ready for the moment. When the moment came, I had paid the price.... It takes a lot of unspectacular preparation to get spectacular results."[107]

PEGGY: In my training diaries I always had a column for preparation. Sometimes that was the only section where I gave myself an A. Maybe my form was off, but I did everything in my power to come to the workout or race prepared–mentally, physically, skill wise, in clothing, my bike tuned up, having knowledge of the course–all those are preparation. When other riders were missing things, like a pair of shoes or a battery for their music, they came to me because it was known I was best prepared and might have a spare of the item they needed.

Imagine you have been training for weeks. One day you are out riding, doing the same thing you have been doing day after day. Let's say you are doing hill climbs with a big gear, and all of a sudden, instead of straining and hurting, the killer climb feels almost easy, and you realize that something good is happening. You are getting fitter and stronger. At that moment, you can feel your confidence grow.

CYCLE WISDOM

"It never gets easier...you just go faster."

—Greg LeMond, U.S.A., Pro World Road World Champion, 3x Tour de France Winner[108]

Being a good racer is a daunting task. However, as you break down the challenge into various parts, what has to be done becomes clearer and seems more and more possible. To excel as a top racer is a matter of developing all technical and tactical skills, and the ability to read the course, weather conditions, and opponents. It's about maintaining awareness and adaptability. To build confidence, mentally rehearse each of these elements, then practice them in training and lesser competitions until you feel: *I can handle this*. Then move on to another challenging part. Work consistently with focus, feeling, and commitment until gradually, you develop the sense that, *yes I can*. Practice the things you have to work on to become a better cyclist. Practice on the course. Practice in practice. Practice with mental rehearsal. Practice until you know you can do it, until you can honestly tell yourself: *I am a strong racer. My finishing continues to improve. I read the race well. I always have good focus.*

EXERCISE 8.2

Confidence Plan

Building a confidence plan will allow you to identify the weaknesses that give you doubts and set goals to improve in those areas.

Design your own confidence-building training program. Always assess and adjust. Identify some parts of racing that challenge you, where you feel your confidence is limited. Think about what elements you have to improve to perform more effectively. Think about what you have to do to really master these elements. Whether it is the road, track, or trails, what would improve your confidence? What self-talk and imagery would help? Act on your commitment and do the practice. Preparation builds confidence. See yourself practicing and improving. Use the tools from previous chapters as you train. Chart your increase in confidence.

Anxiety causes tension and dis-ease. Anxious feelings erode confidence. Some people feel anxious even when they are well-prepared. Remember, feelings affect thinking. To be a positive, confident thinker, one must control emotions. It is difficult to think positive, confident power thoughts when your heart is racing, breathing is shallow, and a voice somewhere in the background is whispering, "Don't screw up." Confidence evolves out of learning how to transform the physical feelings of tension and dis-ease into psycho-physical feelings of ease and power.

CYCLE WISDOM

"You have to sprint on feeling, not thinking. You must have faith in yourself but you cannot think about it too much."

—Jean-Paul van Poppel, The Netherlands, Stage Wins in all three Grand Tour Events, Including Nine Tour de France Stage Wins[109]

CYCLE WISDOM

"Sprinting, mentally, is probably the hardest discipline in cycling because you have to be fearless. If you go 60, 65 into a corner, you look at the shadows, you listen to the sounds, and you see the side of the road, and it's all high speed. It's like being in a traffic jam at 200 km per hour."

—Marc Madiot, France, 2x Paris–Roubaix Winner, UCI WorldTeam Groupama–FDJ Directeur Sportif[110]

The conscious breathing described in the previous section plays a major part in creating feelings of calm, power, and balance. It is a great way to recharge and build confidence. Again, we recommend a few minutes of conscious breathing not just on race days but every day.

To summarize, here are four suggestions to building confidence.

1. Know your job. Know the ABCs, the specific requirements of what you have to do to succeed. Cycle Psyched riders understand the specific behaviors or elements that go into making success possible. And knowing how to acquire or develop these behaviors builds confidence.
2. Confidence also evolves from improving skills—physical and mental skills. Proper preparation includes deliberate practice of the specific skills involved in performing the tasks required. Practice can be both real and imagined. A simple example of how both success and practice (preparation) go together to build confidence is doing repeated hill climbs and noticing power increasing and times getting faster.
3. Along with knowing the job and task mastery, confidence is about creating Right Feeling. The way we are wired as human beings, our feelings affect our thinking and our thinking in turn affects our feelings. Right Feeling comes from having the mental skills and emotional control to deal with the intense feelings generated by the pressure of competition. Emotional management —being in control—requires a special set of psychological skills, skills that can be strengthened with training. Knowing you can control your emotions under pressure is a confidence builder that can lead to significant performance increments.

SAUL: Working with cycling for some time, I came to realize there have been many different ways riders have cheated over the years. These include blood doping, steroids, amphetamines, and something called EPO (a drug that is supposed to increase the number of red blood cells and therefore a rider's oxygen carrying capacity). Immediately before the road race at the Olympic Games, one of the Canadian cyclists approached me, looking less than the picture of confidence. So I asked him, "How are you doing? Are you ready to ride a great race?" His response was not at all reassuring. He shook his head. "How am I supposed to compete with riders who have 25% more red blood cells than I do?" I answered, "Your challenge is to ride a great race. You are competing against yourself, to be the best YOU can be. You have been training for the Olympic road race for YEARS. You are prepared and ready to ride a great race. Do not give away your power focusing on them or on issues you do not control. Focus on what you can do, will do, and that is, to ride with power and speed. You can do that." He looked me in the eye, nodded in agreement, and strode away, appearing a good deal more confident and in control of his destiny. He rode a very good race.

In the challenging world of cycling, some good advice for building confidence, enhancing performance, and well being is: Focus on what you can control. Neurolinguistic programming informs us that if we tell somebody something they don't believe, it can negatively impact their performance. For example, telling a rider to win an Olympic road race, a sprint heat, or a hill climb when they don't think they have a chance, can increase the athlete's tension and have the opposite effect of what is intended. Instead of telling the rider their performance is about winning, one might inspire a better result by encouraging him or her to ride like they can, to be a tiger on the hunt, or to ride hard and make the opposition hurt. These types of challenges are attainable and stimulate more engagement and effort than telling them to go for something they believe is impossible.

Confidence comes from being healthy and in great shape.

SAUL: I had a call from Dana who was rehabbing from shoulder surgery. Her recovery was progressing slowly, and she expressed concerns regarding her readiness for the upcoming season and her desire to have a breakout season with her new team. "I'm just not feeling as confident as I would like to be." I explained that preparation builds confidence, and that she simply wasn't physically prepared to perform at her best. The good news was she had time to heal and was enrolled in what appeared to be a very well-supervised rehab program. I encouraged her to work at her program and with time, she would feel stronger, better prepared, and ultimately more confident.

How do you build confidence? The answer is simple: Improve your preparation and change your focus. Magic happens when you set small incremental goals. Make a commitment, work consistently, run positive programs, mentally rehearse, think power thoughts, keep moving forward, take steps, complete stages, say positive things to yourself, and acknowledge yourself for improving in each element or stage. Nobody is perfect. Remember, when you experience a poor moment, USE IT. Use your mistakes to your advantage. Think of what you can do to improve your performance next time. There is always the next ride. Frame your efforts in a positive light. Use unsuccessful experiences to improve your racing. Use successful experiences to increase your confidence. Then move on to the next element. Chain the elements together. Run positive programs, positive self-talk, and positive imagery on your mental computer.

SAUL: I spent several years consulting with the Los Angeles Rams in the National Football League. One of the high-pressure jobs in football is field goal kicker. A kicker's performance can be affected by confidence. At each practice, the Rams kicker went though a routine to work his skill and build his confidence. He would start by kicking short field goals, or chip shots, from the 15- or 20-yard line. After successfully making two or three kicks in a row, he would move to the 25-yard line. With success at this distance, he would move back farther to the 30-yard line, then the 35, 40, 45, and so on. As he progressed through this regular practice routine, he strengthened his confidence as well as his perception of himself as a competent kicker. Based on what I have observed in every sport, it is clear confidence flows from preparation and success. Do the physical and mental work necessary to experience success in the elements and steps to your ultimate goal. Your confidence will grow and your performance will improve.

Deserving

A sense of deserving is another expression of a confident, winning cycling attitude.

SAUL: When I say a sense of deserving, I am not referring to any sense of entitlement. Rather, I am referring to a confident, aggressive mindset that usually is the product of a lot of hard work. Confronted with a challenge, some athletes just go for it. It's as if they feel they deserve it, and they are going to take it. Most winners have this quality. They expect to be there, and they don't hesitate to go for it. Others do not feel as confident. It is as though they don't expect success, or they need permission to go for it. Sometimes you get the sense that these athletes think too much.

A sense of deserving is a matter of attitude. It is believing you deserve to express your ability: *The opportunity is here for me, and it's mine*. It is part of a predator's mindset. Be the tiger. There is no holding back. Remember, if you don't believe you deserve it, it is unlikely you are going to make it happen.

EXERCISE 8.3

Deserving

Use the following three-step process to strengthen your sense of deserving.

1. Sit back and tune into your breathing rhythm. Allow time for each breath to come all the way in…and go all the way out. Relax. Breathe slowly and smoothly. As you do, remind yourself that you deserve your time. We are not just talking about understanding the idea, but about actually experiencing the feeling of time. As you begin to experience the full time it takes for the breath to flow in and out, acknowledge you deserve your time.
2. Imagine being on your bicycle. Visualize riding well, with ease, speed, and power. As you do, affirm that you deserve to express your power and ability, ALL your ability. Know and feel that you deserve to express all your ability.
3. Bring that awareness and sense of deserving to a race situation. It might be one in which there are more experienced riders; some may even have outperformed you in the past. If you start to feel less powerful and less confident, then use this dis-ease to go deeper into your breathing and acknowledge what you absolutely know to be true, *I deserve to express my ability*. Then bring that sense of deserving into the race.

PEGGY: Once I retired from international racing, I could easily win local races. I knew what moves to make, where to position myself, and when to go. I felt I deserved it and just went for it. I continued to win against national team riders simply by thinking that I had already earned the win based on my previous experience and who I was as a racer.

SAUL: In helping athletes who don't feel deserving or confident about a specific ability, I have found it useful to have them go back to simply feeling deeply relaxed and powerful. We then build step by step from there.

Know that you deserve to express all your ability. Doing the physical, technical, and mental work builds ability, success, and confidence.

HOMEWORK

Boost Your Confidence

1. Outline a plan to strengthen your confidence, using the tools in this chapter.
2. Select two specific challenges to work on and outline how you will improve in these areas.
3. Do the deserving exercise and every day, when you go out to ride think, say to yourself, *I deserve to express all my ability*. Then, like Nike puts it, "Just Do It."

In Chapters 7 and 8, we started a process of developing Right Attitude by continuously choosing to *use* every opportunity to improve and build confidence. In the next chapter, we explore how Identity, Pride, and Love are part of a winning attitude.

CHAPTER 9
Identity, Pride, Love

In this chapter we explore how identity, pride, and love contribute to Right Attitude.

Identity

Identity is another important component in a winning attitude. Your identity is who you think and feel you are, and to a lesser extent, who others perceive you to be. For most of us, our identity evolves with time and experience. Most successful athletes have some identity or image of themselves as effective competitors. Your cycling identity can determine how you behave and perform as a rider. Most importantly, it's something you can shape and control. As we have said before, you get more of what you think about. If you think you can, you may. If you think you can't, you won't succeed. The way you talk to yourself and visualize yourself performing are two important determinants of your self-image. Your cycling identity can give you the energy and confidence that will lift you to excel, or it can act like a weight to slow you down, tire you, and keep you from reaching your potential.

When asked who you are when you are riding at your best, a World Champion responded,

> "I have a smile on my face—My head is on a swivel, fully observing my surroundings—I am consistently near the front —I am moving through the pack at will, taking the wheels I want—I am responding to moves with no hesitation—My

> head is slightly turned to watch the lap board every lap, and I am adjusting my position accordingly."[111]

Socrates said, "Know yourself."[112] It's a good idea since everyone is unique. The performance trick is to find ways to use your strengths and develop your weaknesses. Ride your strengths hard and celebrate your uniqueness quietly.

CYCLE WISDOM

"I can be one of the best climbers if I believe in myself."

—Clara Koppenberg, Germany, TTT World Championship Medalist, UCI World Tour Pro[113]

CYCLE WISDOM

"What is important is to find the particular part of cycling that you are good at—whether it's climbing or sprinting—and use that as the basis of your style. Then you can go ahead and work on your weaknesses."

—Atle Kvalsvoll, Norway, Former Pro Road Racer[114]

CYCLE WISDOM

"Compare yourself to yourself. That's the most satisfying way to achieve improvement."

—Mary Jane Reoch, U.S.A., Hall of Fame Cyclist, Coach[115]

Identity is one of the most important ingredients in winning.

SAUL: An identity image of who you are and how you can and should perform can move you to do things that you think yourself physically incapable of doing. Conversely, wearing the self-image of a loser or a choker can be limiting. Our identity can lift us to superior performances, or it can slow us down and limit us. I asked Hugo Houle, why is it that in Quebec and Canada, where there are a lot of people who love cycling and have dreams of competing at the highest level, he is on the World Tour and they are not?

HUGO HOULE: It's everyday hard work and perseverance, and never giving up…and I think you need to believe in yourself. There are always those people who discourage you, criticize you, and can lead you the wrong way if you don't believe in yourself. For myself, what has helped me to succeed is to work every day as hard as I can, and to focus on the things I can do every day to be better. That's how you end up in a position where you can achieve a great deal. And when you're at the top, you still need to have the same commitment because it's easy to slip back when you stop pushing as hard as you did before.[116]

Hugo Houle

PEGGY: The British Women's Team pursuit squad won a bronze medal in the World Championships preceding the Olympics. However, their self-image was that of winners. They considered themselves better than bronze and viewed the World result as a disappointment. So they committed to using that disappointing performance and dedicated themselves to preparing even better, like the winners they saw themselves to be. The result was they won gold at the ensuing Olympics.

SAUL: While working with a group of cyclists in preparation for the Seoul Olympics, I discussed with them a Greg LeMond happening. LeMond was the first North American to win the Tour de France. Shortly after winning the Tour in 1986, he was accidentally shot while hunting with his brother-in-law in California. He had over 35 shotgun pellets in his body and sustained serious wounds to his lungs, intestines, and his one functioning kidney. There was significant blood loss and broken ribs. A lengthy and complex surgical procedure saved his liver and his life. LeMond ended up losing 20% of his body weight. A slow, painful recovery followed. Months later, LeMond was finally able to return to racing. At one of his first races back, it was said he looked terrible, pale and thin. However, when a group broke away from the pack, there was LeMond in the break with them. I remember asking the racers present, how was it possible that LeMond, who had almost died months prior and was clearly not in top form, could be in the breakaway group? Gervais Rioux, a Canadian National Team member, responded, "Because that's where he thought he belonged."[117] Remarkably, LeMond went on to win two more Tour de France titles in 1989 and 1990.

Our identity, our sense of self, where we think we belong, all have a profound effect on how we perform and handle life's many challenges.

The iconic Greg LeMond.

CYCLE WISDOM

"As long as I breathe, I attack."

—Bernard "The Badger" Hinault, France, Pro Racing Great, 5x Tour de France Champion, Multiple Wins in Vuelta a España and Giro d'Italia[118]

Identity is not a static entity. Identity is something that has been formed over time and by experience, and it can be reshaped. You can change your identity by changing your mind.

In his book *Ask a Pro*, Phil Gaimon responds to someone asking the question, "I'm trying to figure out what kind of rider I am. What determines whether a pro is a sprinter, climber, or time trialist?"

> "I'd guess the answer boils down to genetics. If you are 5 feet tall, 90 pounds with big lungs and slow-twitch muscles, no matter how much you like sprinting and train for it, you're only going to suck. Folks enjoy rides where they are going to beat their friends.... If you want to determine what type of rider you are, sign yourself up for a hard race and see if you get dropped on climbs, flats, or surging, technical sprinting parts. Wherever you get dropped most, you're the other kind of rider."[119]

When queried, "The juniors are coming up, and you've won the World Juniors. If you could give one tip to a junior, what's the one tip you would say to a future Olympian and future World Champion?" Chloe Dygert responded,

> "Don't let anybody define what they think you're good at. You ride how you want to ride. You figure out on your own what you're good at. You're so young still.... Just ride. Figure it out on your own."[120]

Ride your own race!

PEGGY: I love how Olympic road champion Anna Kiesenhofer did just that—she rode the race the way she wanted to, based on her strengths as a time trialist. She went out strong from the gun, leading a small breakaway group of lesser-known riders that gained over 10 minutes on the complacent field of legends. Kiesenhofer then attacked her group and time trialed the final 40 km solo, for one of the biggest upsets in women's cycling. "I planned to attack at kilometer zero, and I was happy I could get in front. That is something I could not take for granted because I am not good at riding in the peloton." She rode the race on her own terms, true to herself, not waiting for the larger, stronger teams to dictate the race. *VeloNews* commented, "Kiesenhofer's story is one that defines the Olympic dream, where a relative unknown can emerge and take glory from a field of favorites."[121]

The word repent comes from the French word *penser*, to think. To repent means to think again. We tend to associate repentance with a particular kind of mind change, with making a commitment to stop sinning. Well, when you think negative things about yourself, you create a loser's identity, and that is a form of sinning. It is limiting and a signal that it's time to rethink. Change your mind. Shift. Becoming Cycle Psyched means creating a positive self-image. Remember, you are the boss, and attitude is a matter of choice.

In Chapter 3, we discussed positive thinking exercises.

1. Regularly repeat, think, and know, *I am a good cyclist.* Know your strengths.
2. Reflect: "When I perform at my best, I…" Know and imagine the specific things you do when you are riding your best.
3. Affirm you are a strong, smart, Cycle Psyched rider. Use positive power thoughts to define and strengthen your identity. Your affirmations and power statements should represent who you are and what you aspire to be. Your identity should be a balance of truths, affirmations, and power statements.
4. Balance your drive to excel with respecting yourself and valuing what you have achieved.

The following bit of wisdom from Svein Tuft makes the fourth point clear.

> "One of the problems for a lot of young riders is the need to break the cycle of who they want to be and what they are trying and struggling to become, and really look into the psychology of what's going on and who they really

are. Many riders are living and performing in a survival mode and in toxic mental mind state. They are struggling to hang on to a dream, and they are in a place where they are not making the best and healthiest decisions. Many need to come to terms with who they are as a cyclist and change their mindset to becoming a role player, a domestique, and accepting and being satisfied with the role of doing everything they can for the team leader.

We all want to dream big. However, one may simply not have the mindset and physiology that match their dream… it's important to accept that reality. Learn to be comfortable with self, to accept yourself and what you are capable of doing well, and appreciate doing what you are good at. Be proud of that. Be happy with your niche in the sport.

However, way too often the ego wants more. And we are driven by social media and want the attention and praise of others. What makes it more challenging is that a pro team environment can be a meatgrinder, one that doesn't really care about you…only about results, results, results. Many teams drive the joy and success out of people and create a high stress environment where riders end up trying to one-up each other.

In life there are certain reality checks. At 40 I was not the same rider I was at 25 or 30. Even though I trained harder. It's important in life to face reality and understand your abilities and your circumstances. Something that has really helped me to accept my reality is the environment I was in and the people in my life. For me it goes back to my good early environment, to hiking and climbing with my dad, and early values learned. Thereafter, I always had a run of like-minded people, who had similar values, people I wanted to be around who weren't doing drugs and self-destructive, crazy things. And for the last eight years of my career, I've been fortunate to be on a good team, with good people. That makes a difference. Not all teams are like that.

Bottom line, my advice is to do what feels good in your heart and soul. Create a role for yourself you are comfortable with. If I had lived on the edge every year, operating in a survival mode, not knowing whether or not I would have a job next year…I would have left professional cycling years ago and moved on to other challenges and another field of self-expression."[122]

Svein Tuft, World Championship silver medalist in time trial.

Kevin Field, race director and head of performance strategy with the Canadian Cycling Association, agrees with Tuft's comment. He encouraged riders to embrace their role as a domestique or team player, and to appreciate the commitment, talent, and work ethic, and take pride in it. "Pro cycling teams can and could do considerably more to respect and value their team players and create a true winning team culture."[123]

Tuft's teammate, Brandon McNulty, concurs. "Svein is a legend, and it was great to have him around. He had a huge wealth of knowledge and experience, and the team always raced best when he was there."[124]

Most World Tour teams value the character and the role played by all team members. As mentioned in Chapter 2, Sylvan Adams, one of IPT's owners, underlined the importance of selecting riders of character. "Cycling is very much a team sport, wherein riders are expected to subordinate their personal results to those of the team's goals, including supporting the team's race leader. This also requires a rider to give his absolute best…absolutely emptying the tank when required. Such special domestique riders are highly coveted by teams, nearly as much as the stars who win the races."[125]

A good example is the career of Alessandro De Marchi. For 11 years as a professional, De Marchi's place was always off the front and in the wind, and usually off the podium and out of the prizes. So more than a few were surprised to see the then Israel Start Up Nation rider wearing the pink jersey in the 2021 Giro d'Italia. "I feel a bit disoriented, almost out of place. I was maybe too used to trying, too used to never giving up, but still never picking up the big prize." De Marchi has claimed just five victories in his 11-year career (including 3x stage wins in the Vuelta a España), but as a rider, he has been appreciated for his honest effort more than for his rare wins.

> "With my style of racing, I know the chances of winning are always low, and the important thing is not to give up. My way of doing things is a lot more romantic than modern cycling allows.... I've always been generous in my efforts, but I don't think it's been a mistake for me to race like that. There have been races where I spent the day in the break and got caught...and I was still happier with those than races where I got a placing."[126]

EXERCISE 9.1

Create An Identity Statement

Prepare your own personal identity statement: Write who you are and could be at your best. Affirm all your strengths and highlight your potential. If you haven't yet manifested a desired quality, incorporate it into your identity statement. If you are truly uncomfortable saying to yourself, *I am a very good cyclist*, then say, *I am becoming a very good cyclist.* Read this statement to yourself and repeat it often. Let it become you.

Psychologists who do intelligence testing know that the absence of a high score doesn't necessarily mean a lack of ability. It simply means the person being tested didn't perform well on that day. When you have a poor ride or a poor race, don't latch onto that disappointing perception and keep rerunning that as an identity program of who you are. Don't let a bad start become a bad race.

Instead, use it. Change your program. Take a breath and say to yourself, "That's not me." Then imagine riding well, being smart, quick, and generally performing well. To improve your performance identity (and increase your confidence), think about and visualize yourself at your best, then work toward making it a reality.

For too many athletes, their sense of well-being is determined by how they perform. If they do well, they feel good about themselves. If they perform poorly, they feel terrible or worthless. It is normal for people who are highly motivated and who work very hard to achieve certain performance goals to be disappointed with poor performance. However, it is important to stay focused on your commitment. Remember and affirm that you are on a positive track and that nothing can take you off that track. If you have a good workout, ride, or race, acknowledge yourself. Rerun your highlight reel, either on video or with mental rehearsal imagery. Repeat your positive self-statements and power thoughts. If you have a poor workout or race don't let that shake your confidence. Again, use it, say, "That's not who I am," and then see yourself riding great.

PEGGY: Sometimes athletes weigh themselves down with expectations. They have an identity that is tough to maintain. They want to win, all the time, and not winning is failing. Take racers who win world titles at a very young age. Sometimes they flounder, unable to find that winning formula again. They become negative and self-critical because they expect themselves to always perform at that super elite level. This pressure is not at all helpful. Instead, focus on process. Working with and strengthening those Right Focus and Right Feeling attributes will lead to performing well, and feeling good about yourself as a cyclist and a person.

Pride

Pride—most cyclists have heard the word and many coaches often use it to rally their athletes. A 14-year-old rider was asked, "What does pride mean to you?" Without a moment's hesitation, she replied, "It's feeling good about what I do." Pride is a composite of many qualities of a winning attitude. It is related to commitment, confidence, identity, and self-esteem. Pride is having a positive sense of who you are, how you choose to represent yourself, and what you have accomplished.

How do you build a sense of pride? There is no simple answer. Many things go into developing a sense of pride, including the way a child is brought up, their values, work ethic, life experience, and self-esteem. And everyone is different. What inspires some people may be completely different from what motivates others. Some people feel proud when they win; others feel pride for competing well.

PEGGY: It doesn't matter who you beat or what you win, it's over when you cross the line. To continue to be happy with your performance you have to compare yourself to yourself. I remember when Saul first saw my apartment, he asked where my medals and trophies were. Many successful athletes have theirs on display. Athletes tend to judge their self-worth based on their results, but because bike racers often compete more often than athletes in other sports, we tend to move on to thinking about the next race rather quickly and do not dwell much on the past. Saul reminded me it's important to take the time to enjoy good performances, to display some of your winning medals and mementos. Sometimes bike races present jerseys, like the Tour de France's yellow jersey. I now have my National Champions jerseys, race winner jerseys, and World Championship bronze medal framed and displayed. They remind me of what I accomplished and can share with upcoming racers. It brings up good feelings and reminds me of my "place" in cycling.

Here are two examples of athletes commemorating their achievements.

Peggy Maass Labiuk's World Championship pursuit medal, framed with articles and photos.

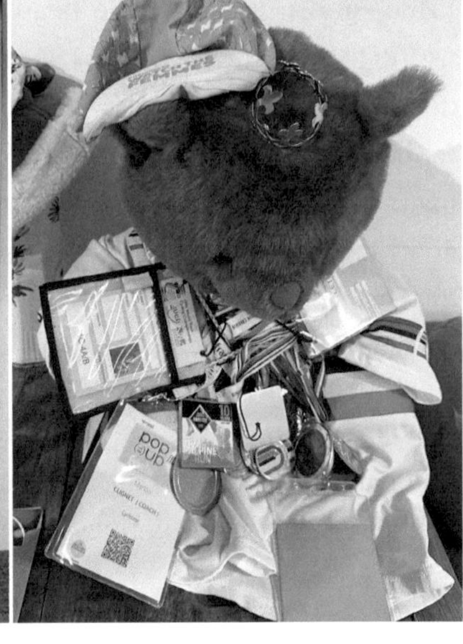

Marion Clignet's Berlin World Championships bear Albrecht, sporting her medals, jerseys, and credentials.

EXERCISE 9.2

Building Pride

1. Relax and breathe. Relaxed conscious breathing can improve the quality of your thoughts and images. Now, begin to think about and imagine yourself racing to the best of your ability, really playing well. Visualize the good stuff.
2. Make the commitment to be the best you can be. Affirm you are willing to do whatever it takes to be the rider and teammate you aspire to be.

3. Do the work to make it happen—in the gym and on training rides. Combine that with mental training. Be consistent. Work at it every day. Give 100 percent every race.
4. Evaluate your progress. Find something positive to acknowledge, even if it's just your dedication and work ethic. Find some area that needs more attention, and improve on it. Work to strengthen what you are good at, and consistently work on the things you need to improve.
5. Walk your talk. Model your commitment and determination to your teammates. Respect yourself in your relations with others.

Abuse, Respect, Pride

In our dealings with others, we often come across people who are kind, caring, supportive, and respectful. Unfortunately, athletes sometimes have to deal with toxic and abusive relationships with coaches, cycling staff, and teammates. These abusive relationships can include both physical and verbal aspects. Verbal abuse involves being exposed to negative, demeaning, and hateful comments. At times, abuse can be sexual in nature. It takes courage, pride, and a sense of self-respect to speak out about abuse. Young cyclists trying to make a team are in an especially vulnerable position. Being excited and new to the team, many don't want to rock the boat and are reluctant to speak up and say anything about a coach, team director, doctor, or a masseur behaving inappropriately and being abusive.

Maggie Coles-Lyster was exactly in that position as a young rider. She had just signed on with an elite European team and was excited to be racing in Europe with the group. Right after her first race, she was sexually abused during a massage by a team assistant acting as a soigneur. The same thing happened after each post-race massage for the week she was there. When she mentioned the situation to teammates, some claimed they had experienced something similar. Coles-Lyster is an excellent cyclist and a positive, proud, young woman. When she returned home to Canada after the race series, she knew she had to speak up. And she did. She spoke with the team director, then wrote an article describing the abuse and her response to it. The article was published in the *Canadian Cycling Magazine* and can be read in the Appendix of this book.

Abuse (physical and verbal) is one of those very unpleasant and challenging situations one sometimes is forced to experience in life. How we deal with it often reflects our courage, self respect, and pride.

PEGGY: I know it's easy to say this when you are not in a compromising situation like the one Maggie describes so well, however, I know I would need to speak up and put a stop to it. I would not respect myself if I allowed something like that to continue. I would get depressed if I did.

Love

Last but not least, love the sport. In describing a Cycle Psyched mindset, we talked about running positive power programs. Using positive empowering thoughts, images, and attitudes to generate energy, emotion, and direction will help you perform at your best. You have a personal connection to an unlimited source of energy in the form of power words and high-performance images that you can use to enhance your game. Remember, attitude is a matter of choice, and you are the boss. A good athlete needs the head, the body, and the heart to succeed. Train the head and the body. Love the sport and love the challenge it provides.

SAUL: I want to add a power word to the list of suggestions that you received earlier. I encourage you to use the word and see how it can be useful for you. The power word I want you to add is *love*. Love is an antidote to fear. Fear is the most limiting program that people run on their mental computers, and it has many faces–fear of failure, fear of embarrassment, fear of not meeting expectations, fear of letting the team down, fear of getting hurt, fear of losing control, fear of the unknown, and even fear of success. Fear causes tension, cuts down breathing, reduces energy flow, and ultimately limits performance. Love is more powerful than fear. It is expansive and opens us to new possibilities. Although fear can motivate a good performance, love can inspire great performances. Love is one of the most powerful forces available to us as human beings. When we combine love with talent and training, remarkable things can happen. Interesting? Perhaps. But does it relate to cycling? Absolutely. Love is at the heart of winning cycling and at the heart of the Cycle Psyched concept.

Chris Froome is a remarkable example of determination, pride, and love. His passion for cycling has nurtured his talent and achievement, and it just may lead him back to the podium. Froome experienced a debilitating training accident in 2019 when a gust of wind drove him into a wall at 40 mph, breaking his femur, elbow, and several ribs. Froome has always insisted he can return to the level that saw him win four Tours de France, two Vueltas, plus the 2018 Giro–his last victory. Many riders would have been tempted to call time on their career after such horrific injuries. Most might have thought enough was enough after difficult comeback years, at the age of 36. Froome however, has remained committed to his cause. And why?

CHRIS FROOME: It's just how I feel about cycling. I genuinely love the sport, I love the process of dedication, of training, of trying to get the best out of myself. Since my crash, it's almost as if I went back to being a neo-pro. It certainly hasn't been easy the last three years, and I've had to overcome a lot of challenges. But I'm not missing any motivation, or any will to do it. I'm willing to train just as hard as ever before. Hopefully having the experience of the last 12–13 years will help me get back there.[127]

Chris Froome, Tour du Rwanda.

PEGGY: Crashing is exemplary for using all the Cycle Psyched tools. Many cyclists fear crashing. Unless you shift your thoughts onto what you can do instead, you will find yourself tensing, going slower, getting dropped, making mistakes. Take a breath, use the release reflex, shift your thoughts. When mishaps do happen or injuries or illness take over, it's the love of cycling that will make you persevere.

Kristen Armstrong, coach and 3x Olympic time trial gold medalist, commented in a press release after Chloe Dygert crashed and was unable to continue while defending her World Championship Time Trial title in 2020, "She loves competition, and the thrill of winning is in her DNA, and that will help her heal. She loves to win."[128]

SAUL: Good things flow from a love of the sport and the challenge it represents. That sentiment is echoed by many of the athletes I have worked with. Over and over they tell me that when they ride and race with passion, they feel like a kid enjoying the sport, and they perform at their best.

CYCLE WISDOM

"Winning a stage race is all about time. You cross the finish line and somebody else wins the stage while you're winning the GC. And it's amazing...but it's not the same as crossing the finish line first when you are giving everything in the last moment to beat everyone next to you. When I won the second stage at the Women's Tour my teammates were like, Who are you? You're like a monster when you cross the finish line, but the rest of the time you're this mellow little girl with a bun on the back of her head. Where's that coming from? That feeling, winning a one-day race where everyone goes all in, that tops about everything else."

—Coryn Labecki, U.S.A., 73x National Champion, Tour of Flanders Winner, Stage 2 and Overall GC Winner, OVO Energy Women's Tour[129]

Coryn Labecki celebrating a victory.

Here are two U.S.A. mountain bikers with different expressions of their love of cycling.

> "I don't ride for the money so much or for the fame. I ride for my heart. I'm a soul rider." Steve Cook[130]

> "My mother and I have a difference of opinion. She thinks I should go see a shrink; I think I should buy a new bike." Alex Obbard[131]

Love is power, and people love to ride with cyclists who love the sport. Thinking loving thoughts about racing can change your feelings and make it easier to handle any cycle-tough moment. Your passion for the sport can help you tap a limitless power source.

EXERCISE 9.3

Feel the Love, Love is Power

1. Identify five things you love about cycling. Recall some of the cycling imagery we discussed earlier. Imagine feeling fast, like a rocket off the start line, like a lion on the hunt, passing on downhills, cornering with G-forces. Do you love competing against the best riders, dominating the lesser riders? Do you love being on the edge, pushing the envelope, making that good move? Do you love to win? Do you love challenges?
2. Identify three things that challenge you in the sport. Are you challenged physically, mentally by race starts, decision making, being crowded, climbing, descending with speed? Now, identify at least one thing to love about each of those challenges. Attaching something to love about a challenge reframes it. Love to corner, love

to descend, love to sprint, love to dominate, love to compete, love quality competition, love pushing yourself beyond your limits. Love the challenges that cycling presents.

Competitive cycling is like a mirror. It's an opportunity to learn and to grow, to discover what you have to work on to become a more complete athlete. Many riders push themselves to succeed because of their fear of failure, and they run themselves down when they don't perform well. Fear stimulates action. Yes, it can kick-start you to get going. But the greatest performances come when people go beyond fear and move into the love zone. Go beyond making failure a negative driver. It's stressful and difficult to live like that. Instead, think, *I love the challenge. I don't need to achieve something to be someone*. Think, *I am...and I can.* Be positive about yourself and find something to love in every cycling situation.

CYCLE WISDOM

"You don't suffer, kill yourself, and take the risks I take for money. I love bike racing."

—Greg LeMond, U.S.A., Pro Road World Champion, 3x Tour de France Winner[132]

Peter Sagan said, regarding his greatest strengths,

> "To be able to concentrate well just at the right time. And, I love my job. Most people spend their working day sitting in offices and can only do sport before work or after work, whereas I get to do my favorite sport during my work time. What could be better than that."[133]

CYCLE WISDOM

"If you don't have the passion for what you are doing, you are only going to get so far. I mean, you can work, and work, and work, and it's going to feel like hard work if you don't have that passion. For me personally, just the fact that I loved being on my bike, I loved being in the outdoors, I loved being in nature. It's a pleasure for me to spend six hours on my bike where for a lot of people I know that sounds like torture, sounds like a tough day at the office."

—Chris Froome, Great Britain, 4x Tour de France Winner[134]

Sports psychologist Jim Loehr says, "The extent to which individuals perform in the upper range of their talent and skill largely depends on the success they have creating and maintaining a particular kind of mental climate within themselves."[135] Some of the mental characteristics Loehr lists as necessary for an ideal performance include: being energetically charged but relaxed; having a positive state of mind; exhibiting mental alertness, focus, discipline, and control. We believe these are the cornerstones of confidence, mental toughness, and a winning sense of self that we discuss throughout *Cycle Psyched.*

SAUL: After a few final edits incorporating exemplary cycling performances from the 2021 Tokyo Olympics, Peggy and I decided our book was done. And then I tuned into watching Para cycling at the Izu Velodrome in Tokyo and saw truly inspiring athletic performances. Cyclists missing arms and legs, cyclists who have overcome debilitating illness, blindness, and life-threatening injuries, competing with focus, courage, and speed. Two performances stand out in my mind. One was by Ricardo Ten Argiles, a Spanish Para cyclist who was badly burned at age eight and lost both arms and one leg. I was amazed watching him fly around the track and win a silver medal. Not surprisingly, his philosophy is, "The most important thing is our attitude when we face difficulties."[136]

The other cyclist I was impressed with was Kate O'Brien, a Canadian racer who competed in the 2016 Rio Olympics as a track racer. In 2017, she experienced a horrific, life-threatening accident while cycling, and incurred a serious brain injury, broken ribs, a broken clavicle, two punctured lungs, and lower body injuries. She was told she may never walk again, but with the help of her therapeutic team, was guided back to the bike. Several years later, she is again zooming around the track and winning a Paralympic silver medal. Reflecting on it all, O'Brien commented, "I never imagined that I would get to compete in the Paralympic Games. I wouldn't have believed anyone if they told me that I would. I don't do well with change. But after 33 years on this planet, I am realizing that change is inevitable, and oftentimes, amazing."[137]

These Paralympians present a wonderful life message—change is inevitable and attitude is important in dealing with difficulties. The lesson: adapt and grow.

SAUL: Watching the Para cyclists reminded me of an experience I had some years before, while consulting with Canada's visually impaired tandem cyclists in preparation for international competition. In visually impaired tandem cycling, the front rider, called the pilot, is sighted and is an accomplished cyclist. The rear rider, called the stoker is visually impaired, sometimes completely blind. To better understand what a stoker might experience, I was blindfolded and rode in the stoker's seat. What the stoker must do is pedal as hard and as fast as they can and go with the flow of the bike controlled by the pilot. When riding a bike at speed, there is a natural tendency to lean into the corner. When you are a blind stoker, pumping as hard as you can and the bike is speeding along, there is a tendency as the bike goes into a turn to rebalance the natural tilt, by leaning in the opposite direction. This doesn't work. The stoker who is pedaling as fast as he or she can, has to learn to blindly trust the pilot's lead and go all out and with the flow. It is easier said than done.

Life and sport present many challenges. Watching the additional challenges that these Para cyclists face one has to be impressed with the character, determination, and talent of these amazing athletes, as well as their passion for cycling. They are all winners.

CYCLE WISDOM

"One thing that cycling has taught me is that if you can achieve something without a struggle it's not going to be satisfying."

—Greg LeMond, U.S.A., Pro Road World Champion, 3x Tour de France Winner[138]

CYCLE WISDOM

"It's a little like wrestling a gorilla. You don't quit when you're tired. You quit when the gorilla is tired."

—Fausto Coppi, Italy, 5x Giro d'Italia Winner, 2x Tour de France Winner[139]

HOMEWORK

Identity & Confidence

1. Examine your identity/sense of self and confidence. Think of your strengths as a cyclist and write them down. Consider the elements that make you effective. Make working with these elements part of who you are.
2. Think of one area that you must improve as a competitor and write it down. Consider the elements necessary for you to be competent in this area. List the things you would have to do to improve. Develop a training schedule with steps and stages to improve in this area. As you work on your program, use positive self-talk, power words, and imagery. Bolster your identity as someone who is good.
3. Review and edit your identity statement. Repeat it to yourself at least once a day. Make it a regular part of your training program and preparation.
4. Love the sport. Grow your passion for competitive cycling. Start to use love as a power word in your training. Love is one of the most powerful forces you can have working for you. Love to play. Love to train. Love to compete. Love a challenge. Love to dominate. Love yourself. Love the situation you're in.

Continue working with all your power words and affirmations. Remember, repetition builds strength. If a couple of words or statements don't feel right to you, let them go. Always be looking for new words. Add a new word or drop a word that you're not using or that doesn't seem to have power for you.

Your identity is who you are. It's a distinguishing character or personality of an individual. Cycling can challenge and shape identity. In this chapter, we explored how identity, pride, and love are part of a winning attitude. To further support you in adopting positive changes, we will be looking at Lifestyle in the following chapter.

LIFESTYLE

Albert Einstein—not a competitive cyclist but someone who enjoyed a spin on his bike—said, "Life is like riding a bicycle. To keep your balance [and succeed] you must keep moving."[140] Balance is key to sustaining development. Lack of balance creates stress and problems, especially when cycling. Women's Pro Road World Championship medalist Cecilie Uttrup Ludwig remarked, "Cycling is a very, very tough sport.... It is difficult to choose where you plan to perform and also to get that balance where you can get some days off with your family and with your loved ones—to get that mental energy back to where you're hungry to go out and eating to win."[141]

CYCLE WISDOM

"It's as if everything is connected to the emotion. If you feel comfortable at home and with what's going on in your life, you're stable and everything seems to be going well, many times that's when you perform at your best because you feel free. You don't have anything in your head bothering you. Everything is in balance."

—Hugo Houle, Canada, Tour de France Stage Winner[142]

CYCLE WISDOM

"You have a dream and you work really hard for it, but you keep yourself a bit calm. You need to find a good balance in your life, and how you can do it. Find a relaxed way to do all this. I think this year I feel really stable, good in what I'm doing. I feel like everything comes together. It's just an amazing season for me."

—Demi Vollering, The Netherlands, 5x Classics Winner, Overall GC Tour de France Winner[143]

Lifestyle

As a high-performance athlete, it's vitally important to appreciate the significance of lifestyle in supporting your well-being and your quest for success. By lifestyle, we mean the way you live day to day. That includes diet, exercise, rest and recreation, relationships, and attitude. While there are vast individual differences amongst cyclists, the following are general comments that apply to most cyclists in each of these five areas.

Diet

Individual athletes differ markedly in terms of metabolism, experience, and preference. Some younger athletes feel they can eat anything (and often they do), without noticing it affecting them; more mature athletes tend to have developed an awareness of how the foods they eat affect performance.

SAUL: When I worked in the NFL with the Los Angeles Rams, I remember cringing at the fast food dietary habits of some of the players, e.g., Coke and doughnuts for breakfast. The players' parking lot was filled with high-priced luxury cars and high-performance sport cars, so I used them to draw an analogy: You wouldn't put junk fuel in your car and expect it to perform well, why do you put junk food in a high-performance energy system like your own body? The same applies to competitive cyclists. Would you put lesser components on your bike? Why feed your body with lesser foods?

As a cyclist you probably want foods that will give you energy, clarity, strength, quickness, and endurance. Many nutritional experts recommend a diet rich in complex carbohydrates, high in fiber, low in fat, with a moderate amount of protein. Hydrating, drinking plenty of fluids, is essential. And most experts suggest eliminating or cutting way back on processed and sugary foods. For pre-competition meals, eat something that is easy to digest. Experiment intelligently and find out what works for you. Take stock of the foods you are used to eating and try to recall what has nurtured good performances in the past. One way to keep track of how your diet affects how you perform is to record what you eat in a performance journal. It's important that you do what works for you.

Here is what champion rider Clara Honsinger had to say on the subject of diet.

> "In a shorter race like cyclocross or criterium, I focus on fueling before the race. This means eating sufficient complex carbohydrates, such as whole grains, fruits and vegetables, in the days leading up to the race, and then shifting to easily digestible carbohydrates, like rice or oatmeal, up to 2–3 hours before the race. I also need to make sure I'm hydrating well right up to the start and consuming enough sodium to maintain body fluid."[144]

The importance of a healthy, high-performance diet is appreciated across sports. Fencing Olympian Shaul Gordon observed,

> "While I knew about the importance of nutrition, I never really paid too close attention…until I started getting older. I have a greater appreciation now of the power a healthy diet can have on performance. Especially if you want to take that 'jump' in your athletic career. Whether it be to be more productive during trainings, to gain muscle mass, or to help your post workout recovery, nutrition is key. So is sleep by the way: I think this too is often overlooked."[145]

Many nutritional experts provide similar basic guidelines. Incorporate lean protein into your meals every day. Eat lots of vegetables. Eliminate processed and fast foods. Replace simple carbs with complex carbs. Limit sugary foods. Drink water throughout the day. Daily eating is about making smart choices of whole foods, not focusing on restricting everything. And keep the eye on quality. The higher the quality of food, the better it is for the body. Avoid foods that have long lists of ingredients. A good rule of thumb is if you can't pronounce it, don't put it into your body. Simple, common sense!

CYCLE WISDOM

"A situation that stands out was when I was concerned about our Olympic athletes' eating habits. Several were eating large, sugary desserts every day. Saul, you spoke to them about how a birthday celebration is once a year. Rather than 'no cake,' you highlighted that dessert was something special, to be enjoyed infrequently."

—Barry Lycett, Canada, Olympic Coach[146]

Former pro Phil Gaimon has made cookies his trademark, but even Gaimon savors them in moderation. "Bike racing burns a lot of calories, which meant that between Clif Bars and kale shakes I could still indulge my lifelong love of cookies, but as a pro athlete, I still had to eat healthy. The obvious solution was quality over quantity."[147] Jakub Fisher, a keen recreational cyclist, added, "To avoid temptation, don't keep junk food in the house. If it's around, you'll eat it. If you know you are going to be smart, order the small instead of the large portion. Portion control is helpful compared to outright denial. And drink water not sugar."[148]

Again, a good way to start managing your cycling nutrition intelligently is to keep a record of eating habits for a couple of weeks. Be completely honest. Write down everything. Often our daily eating patterns aren't what we think they are. You might think you're drinking plenty of water, but then, when you write it down, you find that you are drinking far less than you thought you were. Once you see your actual dietary patterns, make appropriate adjustments and observe how they affect the quality of your training and competition.

EXERCISE 10.1

Diet Journal

Keep track of what you eat for at least 10 days. Observe and evaluate what you ingest and decide if you would like to make changes. Outline a plan for any changes and set goals, just like you have with your physical training.

Exercise

Most cyclists get plenty of exercise during the season, and more and more are working out and building strength and fitness all year long. Physical training is a great way to prove the old saying that what you put in (to your training) is what you get out (performance, power, and endurance). Work hard. And understand you are not a machine. Employ balance. Add diversity to your athletic activity. Overtraining can ultimately limit enthusiasm and athleticism. Take time off regularly and find ways to cross-train. Whenever you can, balance activity and rest. And remember: Fitness and strength build confidence and aid concentration.

R and R: Rest and Recreation

Balance is a key to consistent development. Striking a balance between work and rest is essential. Rest is vital to good performance, and it should be quality rest. You can improve the quality of your rest by developing some relaxation or meditation techniques like those presented in previous chapters. As was mentioned earlier, getting enough sleep is extremely important. Just as you schedule time for training, you need to make sure you get sufficient rest and that your sleep needs are met.

CYCLE WISDOM

"You've got to rest as hard as you train."

—*Roger Young, U.S.A., Track Racer, Olympian, Coach*[149]

PEGGY: It's unlikely you can train for more than five weeks without needing a rest break. By the end of five weeks, you may see signs–like injury, illness, lethargy, loss of power, trouble sleeping, negative thinking. The most resistance I get from athletes I coach is adherence to the preventative rest breaks I prescribe in their programs. Rest is crucial to inducing peaks, so once they comply and follow the pattern of training and resting, they enjoy the performance results. They get regular breaks of three or five days, and two weeks after coming down from a peak. Resting is part of the process, it's re-creating, recreation.

Recreation means re-creation. The most popular recreational activity in North America is TV, but TV is neither renewing nor recharging. Balance activity with rest, routine with spontaneity, and do things that are fun. Many distractions surround the sport, especially at the higher levels. Make time to rest and recharge free of distraction and energy-draining activity. Develop a good R-and-R program.

CYCLE WISDOM

"With so much uncertainty in the race schedule (due to the Covid Pandemic), I've just been trying to have fun riding while still keeping some fitness. I've been on the mountain bike a lot too. It's important to keep some fitness but also keep the body and mind stress-free with the possibility of racing extending into November."

—Brandon McNulty, U.S.A., Junior World TT Champion, Giro d'Italia Stage Winner[150]

Some athletes find meditation a calming way to keep perspective. Meditation and wellness guru Jon Kabot-Zinn says,

> "One reason I practice meditation is to maintain my own balance and clarity of mind in the face of such huge

> challenges, and to be able to stay more or less on course through all the weather changes that I encounter day in and day out on this journey."[151]

PEGGY: We all know someone who appears to have an imbalance–all they do is train and race. They are obsessed. The harder thing to do is to assess ourselves and find our own balance. Sometimes the balance isn't achieved daily, or even weekly, but strive for at least a yearly balance of exercise/rest, routine/spontaneity. Victor was a power house. As a young rider, he was fearless and had a great engine. He could pretty much do it all: climb, sprint, jam in the pack, descend with speed.... He was a talent and some thought, in time, he would be competing successfully on the world stage. However, Victor lacked discipline and balance. He enjoyed socializing, partying, and substance abusing. Not surprisingly, his training became irregular, and his performance began to lack the drive and jump he needed to be effective. Victor never became what many of us thought he would be. It's a reminder that talent isn't enough. Along with talent and passion, you need the commitment, discipline, and a healthy lifestyle to really excel. Unless you are a professional cyclist, it's unlikely that you have the excess funds to party with or to support a lavish lifestyle. Instead, what I have observed, are athletes scrimping, like living on peanut butter sandwiches and pasta, and in sparse conditions. Even more frustrating are the athletes that don't look after their equipment. You don't have to have a lot of money to learn how to tune up your own bike or at least keep it clean and the chain lubed. I saw a super talented rider always riding in winter shoe covers to hold her cycling shoes together. Couldn't she approach a sponsor, a bike shop, to cut her a break on a new pair of shoes? How many racers won't miss training to get a needed bike fitting, a massage, or a checkup at the dentist or doctor? These are self-care, self-image issues that can sabotage success.

Relationships

We are social animals. The relationships you have with others are an important part of your life. If you are fortunate enough to have a relationship with someone who supports you and is understanding of your needs, your moods, and your anxieties during the season, remember that the off-season is payback time, and that means it's your turn to spend time and energy nurturing and supporting them.

CYCLE WISDOM

"To boost my mental strength, I defined what was most important in my life. That is that my friends and family were fine and healthy. After all, whether I win or lose a race, in the evening I am still the same person. You can win lots of races and still be unhappy. It's all a question of your outlook on life. Unfortunately, many people are unhappy with what they have."

—Peter Sagan, Slovakia, UCI World Tour Pro, 3x World Champion[152]

After having tremendous success, winning over 160 races and 30 stages of the Tour de France, Mark Cavendish crashed, becoming physically and mentally challenged. "You don't go from being the best in the world to nothing." With the help of a loving family, wise coaching, sport psychology, and a loyal team leader, Cavendish rebuilt himself and came roaring back to win four more Tour de France stages, tying Eddy Merckx's record of 34 Tour de France stage wins. Through this experience, Cavendish learned to appreciate his relationships. "It really brought a human side to what I do for the first point in my career. It made me realize I didn't win alone. I wish

I had known that, and I would go back and do my career again knowing that."[153]

Mark Cavendish

Solo Overall winner of the 2021 Race Across America, Leah Goldstein, had virtually the same nine-person support team as when she was Solo Female winner ten years earlier, in 2011. Valuing them, treating them with respect, and selecting people that cared about her, were key to success. Acknowledging the team's contribution, Goldstein said, "We won, because of the team effort," and "I owe them my life," because it can be life or death in an event that takes 11 days covering almost 3,000 miles, with little to no sleep for rider or staff.[154] According to Support Crew manager Lori Moger Friend, "You're asking people to do very mentally and emotionally challenging things while sleep deprived, while crowded, and hot and sweaty and uncomfortable. I think most people would probably say the sleep deprivation is the worst…and the most shocking part of crewing…but they're both tough." So valuing and thanking your supporters is important. Friend advises, "Just stay calm, just talk softly to people. Tell them they are doing a good job even when things get hard and get messed up. I try to focus on what's going well so they stay positive and proud."[155]

Riders can benefit by being open to meeting people and learning from others, even competitors. Olympic and World silver medalist Nelson Vails says,

> "You have to take advantage of every opportunity. You have to make it happen. I wasn't one of the guys who said, 'Ahh man you don't know what you're talking about.' I'd ask everyone I'd come in contact with, 'How'd you learn how to do that? Where did you get that from?' Those were my questions so I could learn. I would ask these questions about how and why so when I went into a race, I went in knowing, not assuming, what was going on. It's not like I took a win and went and sat down. I had to study it. How did I do that? And how can I do that again? A key thing for me were my parents, my brothers and sisters, everyone

> around me encouraged me and made cycling fun. It was never a regiment of having to do something like a chore. Everyone around me made it fun to do things…and try things. Try racing up the hill—how can you win a race if you don't try to break away? They made it fun, and if you succeeded you learned something and if you didn't succeed you learned from it."[156]

PEGGY: Speaking at a conference of sport medicine providers, I presented a visual of all the people who helped me in my racing endeavors–it was quite a cluster! From training partners, mechanics, doctors, parents, the friend who motorpaced me, colleagues at the gym, massage therapists, sport psychologists, race organizers, teammates, etc. I had so many people to thank and to be grateful for. It was especially helpful to find things to appreciate about teammates or officials that I wasn't particularly fond of, so that I could treat them respectfully.

Jonas Vingegaard, after winning a stage at the Tour de France, reflected, "I would never have been able to do this without them (his girlfriend and daughter)," and after winning the race overall, "I won it for my family, my girlfriend, and for my daughter."[157] After winning a Tour de France stage, Fabio Jacobsen of the Quickstep (the Wolfpack) Team acknowledged, "As a sprinter, you never win alone. You always are relying on everybody's experience. That's how we win and how we howl…. You put your life in people's hands. You have to trust that they are going to give you everything they have."[158]

EXERCISE 10.2

Your Relationships

Make a list of all those people who have supported you and continue to support you on your cycling journey. Then send them a text or a note of appreciation.

Unfortunately, athletes often encounter unsupportive and even toxic and abusive relationships in pursuit of their cycling goals and dreams. These negative relationships can involve coaches, team personnel, teammates, as well as the people who are part of the athlete's personal and social lives. While we have repeatedly stated that if the goal is to be the best you can be, you have to *use* the situation to make yourself better and stronger. However, that can be extremely difficult when it comes to a coach who is abusive and continuously putting you down, or if the people you live with and love treat you poorly. These relationships can be destructive to one's energy and spirit. In the Appendix, we have added a section which deals specifically with the issue of abuse in cycling.

Attitude

Attitude is also very much a part of a healthy, high-performance lifestyle. Again, attitude is a matter of choice, and it is a key component of a healthy lifestyle. Choose to be positive. We talked about having a winning competitive attitude (commitment, confidence, and identity) in Chapters 7, 8, and 9. Two other elements of attitude that we would like to remind you to bring to your daily life are gratitude and love.

SAUL: By gratitude I mean appreciating what you have, and not dwelling on what's missing. Many athletes know people who are sick, disabled, and far less fortunate than they are. Don't sweat the small stuff. Every day, be grateful for your health and energy, and the opportunity to enjoy performing at a sport you love. By love I mean accepting and respecting people and opportunity in your life. Be kind and positive with those you work with and those who support you. And live the golden rule, do unto others what you would want them to do unto you.

Love. Love is power. Love is an attitude and a feeling, and you are the boss. We encourage you to love the challenge cycling presents at every level. Love being healthy and free to get out on your bike and ride. Love cycling as a fitness enhancing experience. Love cycling as an inexpensive, healthy way to get from one place to another. Love cycling as an enjoyable balance to so many things in life. Love cycling as a self-reflection experience. Love cycling as a test of strength and will. Love to ride as a way to challenge yourself, and as a means of competing with others. Love cycling for both the friendship and the solitude it can provide. Love cycling for the feeling of wind in your face and the places it can take you.

Paying attention to diet, exercise, rest and recreation, relationships, and attitude supports your commitment, performance, and self-respect. Elite performers understand this. Effectively managing these areas of lifestyle may take a small percentage of your total effort. Each can be crucial, just like a finishing sprint might be a tiny portion of the time and physical effort of a race, but it can be decisive to the race's outcome.

A QUICK RECAP

Many elite cyclists would agree that focus, commitment, belief, confidence, emotional control, and the ability to deal with fear, frustration, pain, and difficulty, are critical factors in a cyclist's success. This book is a tool to help you manage these factors and be Cycle Psyched.

> **CYCLE WISDOM**
>
> "There are so many facets to performance where psychology has an impact: setting goals, dealing with setbacks in training, managing priorities, and then getting to the start line ready to race with some tactical plans ready to use."
>
> *—Nicole Cooke, Great Britain, Olympic Road and Road World Champion*[1]

CHAPTER 1: The Three Keys

1. The mind is a human super computer, and you are the boss.
2. You get more of what you think about. Think positive.
3. Our feelings affect our thinking. Manage thought and feeling.

The three keys to having a winning mental game are: Right Focus, Right Feeling, and Right Attitude.

CYCLE WISDOM

"The real road race is not on the hot, paved roads, the torturous off-road curves, or the smooth-surfaced velodrome. It's is the electrochemical pathways of your mind."

—Alexi Grewal, U.S.A., Olympic Road Race Gold Medalist[5]

CHAPTER 2: Goals & Self-Assessment

Since our goals drive our performance, it is important to set relevant, meaningful goals: long-term, intermediate, and short-term. Create smart goals. Know your strengths and areas to improve. Continuously assess and adjust.

CYCLE WISDOM

"The most powerful thing you can do is set goals. The most important thing is the mind. That's where the power is, believing in your goals."

—Alison Sydor, Canada, Olympic Mountain Bike Cross-Country Medalist, Cross-Country World Champion, Road World Championship Medalist[6]

CHAPTER 3: Power Thinking

Positive, technical, strategic, and personal thoughts give you and edge. Build mental strength with power words and affirmations.

CYLCE WISDOM

"Your thoughts shape your reality. Think power thoughts like *smooth and fast*, *I can*, and *I corner well*. You get more of what you think about. Positive thought creates positive results. Use power words and affirmations."

—*Peggy and Saul*[15]

CHAPTER 4: High-Performance Imagery

Imagery is a basic mental function. Visualizing yourself excelling can be a powerful aid to enhancing performance and well-being. For Albert Einstein, "Imagination…is the preview of life's coming attractions."[28] Three aspects of high-performance imagery include goal imagery, stimulating imagery, and mental rehearsal.

CHRIS FROOME: For me this is something very personal. I find visualization helps a lot. I am meticulous about planning as well. It really helps me. I'll just give an example: If I know that on stage 10 of the Tour de France we go up this big mountain and that's going to be one of the crucial moments of the race, I have to get there and see it beforehand…see the road, see the bends in the road so I can picture it in my mind. And quite often when I go and do those reconnaissance rides, I'll be able to pick a point on that road where, I'll say,

"Right, this is where I am going to make my move…and this is what's going to happen behind me when I make the move. This guy is going to react like that, that guy is going to react like that, this one won't want to chase me because he's going to expect someone else to do it, so this is the moment to attack." And for weeks before I actually get to that point in the road, that stage in the race, I'll be replaying this video in my mind how I want to see things pan out. And of course, sport is so unpredictable, I could get to that point in the race and I could have a flat tire and I wouldn't be able to execute what I was planning, so there are so many things outside of our control. But sometimes my best performances have come on those days when literally I've got to that point in the road and I've worked myself up so much for that moment where I was going to make the move, or do something that would make a difference in the race, that when I get there, it almost feels as if I'm on autopilot. It doesn't even hurt. The legs don't even hurt even though I'm doing a big effort…or anything…. Generally we would go up there even two or three months beforehand, go to see the roads and the key points in the race. Yeah, and quite often when I go and see these, I'll go see the finish climb of stage 10, or whatever it is, and I'll go and ride it once just to see it, and then I'll go back and ride it again at race speed just to really replicate at that kind of effort. So it basically leaves me with a really good picture of what exactly is required so that's also going to help my training in the weeks leading up to the race so I know what kind of physical effort it's going to take.[37]

CYCLE WISDOM

"I imagine I am an eagle soaring, watching, ready to attack."

—*Peggy Maass Labiuk, U.S.A., 2x National Champion, World Championships Medalist, Ultra Marathon World Record Holder*[32]

CHAPTER 5: Managing Emotions & Conscious Breathing

Cycling is an intense, highly competitive, high-speed sport. To compete successfully, you must be able to manage your emotions, and conscious breathing is key to maintaining Right Focus and Right Feeling. It keeps you in the now, integrating mind and body.

CYCLE WISDOM

"Breathing is definitely a massive one. I think breathing is still not understood 100%, nor are the benefits you can get through breathing exercises. I've certainly found in warming up for a time trial, taking some deep breaths, slowing the breaths down really helps. It helps me to focus on what I really need to do...and it knocks everything else out."

—Chris Froome, Great Britain, 4x Tour de France Champion[43]

CHAPTER 6: Changing Mental Programs

It's important to understand how to create good feelings. It's also important to be able to change a tense, anxious, negative thought into a positive feeling. Release Reflex, Parking It, Turning The Wheel, Sending Power Out, Mastering Pain, and Blowing Off Tension are effective ways to change mental programs.

CYCLE WISDOM

"The key is to be able to endure psychologically."

—Greg LeMond, U.S.A., Pro World Road Champion, 3x Tour de France Winner[50]

CHAPTER 7: Commitment

If you want to excel, you must be resilient and willing to pay the price. If the goal is to be the best cyclist you can be, then you must "use" whatever comes up. If it's positive you use it to build your confidence. If it's negative, use it to improve your process. Winners use everything.

CYCLE WISDOM

"Want to improve...to be the best you can be? Push yourself: you can't get good by staying home. If you want to get, fast you have to go where the 'fast guys' are."

—Steve Larsen, U.S.A., National Team Road Racer[75]

CHAPTER 8: Confidence

Two things build confidence: success and preparation. Regarding the latter, imagine you have been training for weeks; one day you are out riding, doing the same thing you've been doing day after day. Let's say you are doing hill climbs with a big gear; and all of a sudden, instead of straining and hurting, the killer climb feels almost easy, and you realize that something good is happening. You are getting fitter and stronger. At that moment you can feel your confidence grow. It takes a lot of unspectacular preparation to get spectacular results.

CYCLE WISDOM

"I go into every race thinking I'm going to win."

—Chloe Dygert, U.S.A., 8x Track and Road World Champion, Olympic Medalist[101]

CHAPTER 9: Identity, Pride, Love

How you see yourself, how you live your life, and the passion you have for cycling and life, determines the success and enjoyment you will have in the sport.

CYCLE WISDOM

"Compare yourself to yourself. That's the most satisfying way to achieve improvement."

—Mary Jane Reoch, U.S.A., Hall of Fame Cyclist, Coach[115]

LIFESTYLE

As a high-performance athlete it's vitally important to appreciate the impacts lifestyle has in supporting your well-being and your quest for success. Important aspects include diet, exercise, rest and recreation, relationships, and attitude.

CYCLE WISDOM

"You've got to rest as hard as you train."

—*Roger Young, U.S.A., Track Racer, Olympian, Coach*[149]

This concludes the path of Cycle Psyched. Now it's up to you to work this program to make the changes you want. We hope these writings, examples, exercises, and homework empower you to do that. Be smart, tough, and Cycle Psyched…and keep the rubber side down. Best wishes, SAUL and PEGGY.

APPENDIX

Abuse in Cycling

To be successful, an athlete needs a supportive environment in which to train and compete. As we mentioned in Chapter 9, athletes sometimes have to deal with toxic and abusive relationships, the latter being both verbal and physical, and perhaps sexual. Young cyclists, new to a team or trying to make a team, are in an especially vulnerable position and often reluctant to speak up about a coach, team director, doctor, or masseur who is behaving inappropriately and being abusive.

Here is the article by Lily Hansen-Gillis from *Canadian Cycling Magazine*, dated March 6, 2020, titled "Maggie Coles-Lyster's story brings attention to sexual abuse in women's cycling: 'It Makes Me Angry How Many People Think This Doesn't Happen in Cycling.'"

> In April 2017, Canadian cyclist Maggie Coles-Lyster was an 18-year-old junior rider. She had just signed on to race with Lares–Waowdeals (now Doltcini–Van Eyck) a Belgian UCI women's continental team. For her first competition with Lares–Waowdeals, she flew to the Netherlands for a multi-day stage race. "I was super excited to be going to the Netherlands to race with my new team,"

says Coles-Lyster. "The year before, I had gone to Europe for a couple weeks with the national team. It was my first time racing road in Europe and I was immediately hooked on the fast, aggressive racing style." Racing on a European team was a new opportunity for Coles-Lyster. After Day 1 of the stage race, she had her first post-race massage with the team's assistant (who also worked as a soigneur). But instead of relaxing her muscles in preparation for the next day, the experience left her feeling uncomfortable and confused.

A situation no woman should be in: The soigneur had sexually assaulted her during her massage. He continued to sexually assault her during every post race massage session that week. Although there was a language barrier, speaking with some of the other women Coles-Lyster learned that teammates had also experienced the same abuse during his massages.

"I was uncomfortable," said Coles-Lyster, "but I had the opportunity to be on this team. I felt like I had to totally embrace it—not cause a disruption or a disturbance or put it in any kind of jeopardy." During team dinners the soigneur would take photos of Coles-Lyster and text them to her. He would send her intimate messages and take her by the arm before she raced. She didn't know what to do.

Back in Canada: After the race, Coles-Lyster came home to finish her last semester of high school. She was scheduled to return to Europe to race with Lares–Waowdeals that summer. Coles-Lyster knew she would have to live in the same house as the soigneur from July to September and she confided in her parents what had happened on her first trip. They helped her write an email to team director Marc Bracke. "I explained how I was uncomfortable with the inappropriate messages the soigneur was sending," says Coles-Lyster. "I said that I felt the way he was acting with me was unprofessional and that his actions were inappropriate." The email had no effect.

Bracke told her not to be afraid of the soigneur. "He basically blamed it on a language barrier," says Coles-Lyster. "He said he talked to the soigneur and told him to give the riders space. He said that the soigneur understood. That was it. No followup."

Coles-Lyster and her mother began planning how she would handle living in the same house as a man who had sexually abused her. "We would strategize ways of how I would deal with," says Coles-Lyster. "I had to plan what I would do if something happened." In the end, the soigneur was let go for unknown reasons the week Coles-Lyster arrived in Europe.

Coming to terms with what happened, Coles-Lyster says it took her time to process the experience. "Nothing like that had ever happened to me before," she says. "I think it took up until last year for me to actually wrap my mind around it—to just understand and come to terms with what actually happened."

She tried to shove the memory under the rug—forget about it and move on with racing. She continued to grow in cycling and went on to earn a track junior World Championships title, raced for Canadian team Macogep–Argon18, Pickle Juice Pro Cycling and DNA Pro Cycling and she won two track medals at Pan Ams. But in the past year, as women in the cycling world began to come forward with their experiences of verbal and sexual abuse, Coles-Lyster knew she had to share her story.

Not an isolated incident: In February, the UCI opened a formal investigation into Doltcini–Van Eyck Sport women's team. During contract negotiations, Marc Bracke, who is still the director of the team, had asked U.S. cyclist Sara Youmans to send him images of herself "in panties and bras." "Don't be shy," he said. "This is the start of a relationship of trust."

In June 2019, three women from UCI women's team Health Mate Ladies Team filed complaints against the team's general manager Patrick van Gansen. They left the team because of his abusive treatment and inappropriate behaviour. After they filed complaints, six other riders confirmed they had experienced similar situations on the team.

A report released last year by the Dutch Cycling Federation found that more than a quarter of top female Dutch riders said they had felt unsafe in the sport. Thirteen per cent said they had experienced inappropriate sexual behaviour, including touching and comments. "It makes me angry how many people think this doesn't happen in cycling," says Coles-Lyster. "Who knows why that is? Maybe because it's a male-dominated sport, but the number of people who are shocked that this goes on is quite surprising." Coles-Lyster notes that many of these cases happen with young women, who are away from their families, are put in one-on-one situations with adults.

Sexual harassment education: Currently, there are no UCI-mandated sexual harassment seminars. Coles-Lyster thinks that cycling organizations and the UCI need to focus on sexual harassment education at all levels. "We need sexual harassment seminars," she says. "Everybody needs to be educated on what sexual harassment actually looks like. That's the biggest thing, when something like that actually happens to you, you wonder, is this the way massages are supposed to be? As a junior you don't necessarily have the life experience to know what is normal."

Coles-Lyster says that until she publicly spoke about her story, she didn't know what steps to take to report abuse to the UCI. She believes these channels need more visibility and riders need to feel safe going to them. "Sexual harassment is the extreme of it, but organizations and teams need to look at how they treat women," says Coles-Lyster. "They need to strive for equality between women and men and create equal opportunities for both."

A necessary conversation: "As a female in such a male-dominated sport—really just as a female in sport in general —when this happens your career is really your first thought," says Coles-Lyster. "What are the repercussions? What will people say? How could this affect me in my career?" Her goal in coming forward with her story was to spark a conversation. "The more people who talk about this, the more stories that will come out and the more action that will hopefully be taken."

So far, Coles-Lyster says the outcome has been positive. "It's been super empowering," she says. "The connections it's created between other female cyclists and supporters of the sport is what needs to happen. I just really hope this will just inspire and empower more people to come forward with their own stories."

In addition to sexual abuse reported above, there are several other forms of abuse that athletes experience, such as physical abuse, social abuse (e.g., isolation), and most commonly, verbal abuse. The latter is usually caused by insensitive, negative, bullying coaches who often don't realize the impact their coaching style has on their athletes. Young athletes are particularly vulnerable to coaching abuse. They often lack maturity and if they are new to the team or sport, reluctant to voice criticism regarding the way they are being treated for fear of being rejected.

Abuse in any form is highly stressful and can significantly and negatively impact performance and well-being. Along with addressing the authorities about any abuse, the same techniques we have presented in this book—Right Focus, Right Feeling, and Right Attitude—can help in coping with stress of the abuse.

For example, if someone was being repeatedly criticized by a negative, bullying coach, one can either *use it* to assertively affirm their self-worth as an athlete and person, or it can use them. If one is able to *use it* by aggressively talking to themselves in a positive manner, reaffirming their talent, potential, and self-worth, and at the same time working diligently with conscious breathing to create and strengthen feelings of calm and power, they can turn an unpleasant, challenging situation into one that builds character and mental toughness.

Indeed, the very same techniques we have outlined to enhance cycling performance can and should be applied to dealing with abuse in any form, and to generally improve the quality of one's life.

ABOUT THE AUTHORS

Dr. Saul L. Miller is one of North America's leading sport and performance psychologists. He is the author of ten books including: *Performing Under Pressure, Why Teams Win, Hockey Tough: A Winning Mental Game, Winning Golf: the Mental Game*, and *Sport Psychology for Cyclists* which he wrote with Peggy Maass Labiuk in 1999. Dr. Miller consults with sport, corporations, and health organizations across North America and Europe. He has worked with the New York Mets, Los Angeles Dodgers, Rams, Clippers and Kings, Seattle Mariners, Florida Panthers, Vancouver Canucks, Nashville Predators, plus numerous European pro teams, PGA Tour golfers, and Olympians and national athletes from the U.S., Canada, Russia, Switzerland, Slovakia, and Italy in over 30 different sports. Dr. Miller has been consulting with elite cyclists from Canada and the U.S. for over four decades. A graduate of McGill University and the Institute of Psychiatry, University of London (Ph.D. Clinical Psychology), his work reflects his study of Eastern disciplines, Western psychological thinking, and over 40 years of front-line experience consulting with the world's top performers.

Peggy Maass Labiuk is a former U.S. National Team road and track racer, who excelled by being tough, smart, and psyched. She shares her cycling acumen as a World Championships medalist (individual pursuit), 2x National Champion (criterium, kilometer), and world record holder (24-hr endurance record, 490.5 miles, human paced) in anecdotes and coaching notables. Her success in such a broad range of events (track, road, U.S. Olympic, and World Championships teams) and having coached from club to elite levels (British National Women's Endurance Squad) led to the practical execution of the sport psychology plan presented in *Cycle Psyched.* While Labiuk now rarely competes, she coaches, trains on the velodrome, and still scores some Strava segment QOMs.

PHOTOGRAPHY CREDITS

Dedication page: Shaima Nasiri, thank you to the unknown photographer in Vancouver, B.C., who captured this fabulous shot.

Page 3: John Pierce, PhotoSport International

Page 13: Vic Armijo, RAAM Media

Page 27: Israel Premier Tech

Page 53: Brendan Cleak

Page 54 top: John Pierce, PhotoSport International

Page 54 bottom: Vecstock, freepik.com

Page 92: John Pierce, PhotoSport International

Page 106: Richard DeGarmo

Page 126: John Pierce, PhotoSport International

Page 135: Dave Mendenhall

Page 147: John Pierce, PhotoSport International

Page 167: Israel Premier Tech

Page 169: Richard DeGarmo

Page 173: John Pierce, PhotoSport International

Page 178 left: Peggy Maass Labiuk

Page 178 right: Marion Clignet

Page 182: Israel Premier Tech

Page 183: John Pierce, PhotoSport International

Page 200: John Pierce, PhotoSport International

Page 226: Nicole Cooke, Simon & Schuster

Page 231: Richard DeGarmo

CONTRIBUTORS

Almost all information on the impressive cast of contributors is easily accessible on the internet (Wikipedia, team and individuals websites and blogs), but details are provided here for easy reference, in alphabetical order.

Sylvan Adams: a philanthropist and a champion cyclist. On the bike, Adams is a 2x World Masters Champion, 6x Canadian National Champion, 17x Quebec Champion; won four Pan-American gold medals, and a total of five golds at the 2009 and 2013 Maccabiah Games. All that, and he only began racing in his 40s. Adams has generously supported cycling and is responsible for bringing stages of the Giro d'Italia to Israel in 2018, building a velodrome in Tel Aviv, helping the Afghan women's cycling team escape Afghanistan, and founding the Israel Start-Up Nation cycling team, now Israel–Premier Tech.

Alex Amiri: young Canadian who is the son of coach Houshang Amiri. In his first international race in Romania (Tour of Sibiu), the work he did for his team (Team California) earned him the combativity prize. His personal achievement highlight is his 4th place overall at the Cascades Cycling Classic (2019) as well as KOM jersey winner at the San Dimas Stage Race.

Kristen Armstrong: 3x Olympic gold medalist in time trial 2008, 2012, and 2016. A former swimmer, runner, and triathlete, Armstrong focused on cycling due to osteoarthritis. She has a long list of National and World Championships medals, as well as Pan Am Games podiums from 2002–2016. Known for her attention to detail, she and her spouse started a bike parts company, and she became performance director for U.S.A. Cycling in 2017. She is not related to Lance Armstrong whose former wife was also named Kristen.

Erin Attwell: a Canadian track racer whose pursuit squad (with Maggie Coles-Lyster) won bronze in the Pan Am Games in Lima, Peru, in 2019. She is a former Junior National Road Champion and has been named to the NextGen National Development Team while being a pre-med student. The team pursuit squad won gold at the 2023 Pan American Track Cycling Championships.

Marie-Claude Audet: former Canadian National Team cyclist, competed in the first Olympic road race for women, in 1984.

Steve Bauer: an excellent sprinter, the first Canadian to win an Olympic road race medal (silver in 1984), subsequently turning pro and earning a World Championship road race bronze medal in only his second professional start. Bauer was teammates with Bernard Hinault and Greg LeMond and placed 4th in the Tour de France after winning a stage and wearing the yellow jersey for five days. In all, he raced the Tour 11 times and wore yellow 14 times. He narrowly missed winning the Paris–Roubaix classic, in a photo finish that is still the closest in the history of the race. After racing, Bauer founded Steve Bauer Cycle Tours, initiated the first Canadian-based pro team, and was recently named head sports director of Israel–Premier Tech Pro Team.

Edward "Eddie B" Borysewicz: a Polish racer and National Champion. He became the first full-time coach for the U.S. Cycling

Federation in 1977. He groomed Greg LeMond and was proactive in coaching women—Americans Sue Novara, Connie Paraskevin, Connie Carpenter, Rebecca Twigg, Cindy Olavarri, Mindee Mayfield, and yours truly (Peggy) won World Championship medals and titles under his tutelage. The 1984 Olympic Games in Los Angeles marked his effect with eight medals won by the U.S. team. Borysewicz's Polish accent and sayings endeared him to many.

Cassie Campbell: 2x captain and Olympic gold medalist for Canada in women's ice hockey, in 2002 and 2006. Post career, she became the first female color commentator on the *Hockey Night in Canada* show. Inducted into the Order of Canada, Campbell is well known as a role model and for her charity work.

Mark Cavendish: still chasing the record for most Tour de France stage wins, having tied Eddie Merckx with 34. "Without the TdF, cycling doesn't exist. Even before I rode the TdF, I was obsessed with it. These bike riders suffering these horrible distances for three weeks in July. It's addictive. It's savage but so beautiful, so beautiful. We race 21 stages, over 3,500 kilometers. A rider wins one stage of the TdF, it makes not just the year—[it makes] their whole career."[159] Cavendish has racked up 54 Grand Tour wins (3rd all time) and 162 pro wins (2nd all time), was World Road Champion in 2011, as well as succeeded on the track including Madison World Champion in 2005 with partner Rob Hayles.

Maggie Coles-Lyster: the Canadian star won a rainbow jersey as a junior in the points race in 2017, a bronze in the team pursuit at the Pan American Track Cycling Championships in 2018, silver in both the team pursuit and Madison in the Pan Am Games in 2019, and a bronze medal in the 2021 Commonwealth Games. She won the Canadian National road race in 2022. Successful in both road and track, Coles-Lyster is currently aiming for the next Olympic Games.

Steve Cook: American pro mountain bike racer of the 80's, part of the first class inducted into the Mountain Bike Hall of Fame in 1988. He furthered the sport creating a single-track trail network in the National Forest around Crested Butte, Colorado.

Nicole Cooke: first cyclist to win both the Olympic gold and World Championships road race in the same year, and first female cyclist from Great Britain to win an Olympic gold. Cooke was also Junior World Champion in time trial, 2x road race, and mountain bike cross-country. She won 54 UCI one day races and 27 classics in her career. Normally an athlete outside of the limelight, she spoke out against doping in the sport, and after her retirement, authored an autobiography *The Breakaway: My Story*. She is known as a trailblazer in creating opportunities for women in cycling.

Calvin Coolidge: 30th President of the United States, a lawyer and conservative Republican. He was born in Vermont, served in Massachusetts in the roaring 1920s, and was known for his frugality.

Fausto Coppi: Italian who won the Giro in 1940, 1947, 1949, 1952, 1953, and the Tour in 1949 and 1952. Add to that the World Championships title in 1953. More notable results include winning 5x Giro di Lombardia, 3x Milano–San Remo, as well as winning Paris–Roubaix, La Flèche Wallonne, and setting the hour record (45.798 km). There is a lot more to the story of "The Heron" during the war, his rivalry with Bartoli, a love affair, and a tragic ending.

Larson Craddock: American pro road and track racer, known for finishing the Tour de France in 2018 despite incurring a painful injury on the opening stage. Awarded the Lanterne Rouge for being the last place finisher. Craddock turned his demise into a fundraiser for the Houston velodrome, flooded by hurricane Harvey. In the 2021 Vuelta a España, he led out teammate Magnus Cort for the win and celebrated crossing the line with his arms raised.

Alessandro De Marchi: Italian who has been track racing since 2007. As a pro he regularly wins stages in the Grand Tours and classics and held the leaders jerseys in the 2021 Giro. In the 2022 UCI Gravel Championships, he placed 7th.

Chloe Dygert: began her cycling stardom with double gold as a junior at the World Championships in 2016, winning both the individual time trial and the road race in Richmond, Virginia. She was recruited for the track program and won multiple World Championship titles and two Olympic medals. In 2019, she won the World Championships individual time trial on the road and came in 4th in the road race. She is pursuing both disciplines and overcoming injuries. Dygert won the 2023 U.S. National women's pro road race, time trial, and World Championships pursuit and time trial on her road to full recovery.

Albert Einstein: won the Nobel prize in Physics in 1921. German-born physicist who came to the U.S.A. in 1933. There is much more to read about his research, theories, and quotes.

Kevin Field: head of performance strategy at Cycling Canada. *Canadian Cycling Magazine*'s story "The Moneyball of Canadian Cycling" by Dan Dakin, September 8, 2019, gives a detailed account of how Field uses data, analytics, and camaraderie to support racers to be successful. Field was behind the breakthroughs of Sven Tuft, Michael Woods, the Canadian women's track team and junior road championships medalists.

Jakub Fisher: An enthusiastic recreational cyclist in Vancouver and an insightful optician.

Chris Froome: 4x winner of the Tour de France, 2x winner of the Vuelta a España, winner of the Giro d'Italia—some in the same year and making modern-cycling history. Froome was born in Kenya and started racing in South Africa. He was scooped up by Great Britain's National Team and became a member of Team Sky. Froome suffered a potentially career-terminating injury in 2019. Despite significant challenges, he has battled back and found the podium again in the 2022 Tour de France.

Jakob Fuglsang: Born in Switzerland but races as a Danish professional, previously a mountain bike Under-23 World Champion. He won multiple Danish time trial Championships, was 7th overall in the 2013 Tour de France, assisted Vincenzo Nibali win the 2014 Tour. He won silver in the 2016 Olympic road race. His breakthrough career win was the 2017 Critérium du Dauphiné. He won it again in 2019, as well as the Vuelta a Andalucia and Liège–Bastogne–Liège. 2020 brought another Vuelta a Andalucia title and a first in the Giro di Lombardia. He has many other top performances.

David Gaudu: won the Tour de l'Avenir in 2016 and is holding his own in the pro ranks. The French rider has stage wins in the Vuelta, Critérium du Dauphiné, Tour de Romandie, Volta ao Algarve em

Bicicleta, Tour de Luxembourg, and placed 4th in GC in the 2022 Tour de France.

Phil Gaimon: former pro from Columbus, Ohio, raced for Jelly Belly, Kenda Gear Grinder, Bissell, Garmin–Sharp, Optum–Kelly Benefits Strategy, Cannondale, and finally the U.S. National Team pursuit squad. After a horrific training crash in 2019 ended his racing career, Gaimon set out on another path. Using his writing skills and social media, Gaimon has built a following by authoring several entertaining cycling books and creating a YouTube channel documenting "The Worst Retirement Ever." He travels to challenge Strava segments, especially hill climb KOMs (King of the Mountains).

Felice Gimondi: despite racing during the years Eddie Merckx dominated, Gimondi's wins place him in the top 10 of all time. He won the Tour de France at age 22, filling in for a teammate and having to get his mother's permission to ride. Two years later, in 1967, he won the Giro, and again in 1969 and 1976, making him an Italian hero. He won the Giro, the Tour de France, and the Vuelta—cycling's Triple Crown—making him a cycling legend. He even won the grueling Paris–Roubaix and in 1973, beat Merckx for the World Championships title. Gimondi passed in 2019 at the age of 76.

Missy Giove: won 14 NORBA downhill titles, three overall NORBA downhill crowns, 11 World Cups, two World Cup overall crowns, and the 1994 World Championship title. She was famous for racing with a necklace bearing the desiccated body of her deceased pet piranha, Gonzo. Peggy remembers hearing Missy at races, imitating the sound of motorbikes revving.

Leah Goldstein: truly a phenomenon. She was World Kickboxing Champion, then a 10-year veteran of the Israeli Commandos and Secret Police Force and an Israeli duathlon champion, before returning to Canada and becoming a world-class cyclist. Goldstein then turned her focus to the Race Across America and became the first woman to be the overall solo RAAM winner. Her story is told in her book *No Limits* and a documentary of the same title. Goldstein, who keeps pushing the limits, was accepted to be the first woman to ride the 5,600-mile Red Bull Trans–Siberian Extreme, the longest race in the world.

Shaul Gordon: Canadian Olympic fencer in the sabre discipline, NCAA All American, and Pan American Games multiple medalist.

Forest Gregg: American pro football Hall of Fame and coach. Gregg won five NFL Championships with the Green Bay Packers under Vince Lombardi and one Super Bowl win with the Dallas Cowboys. He was head coach with numerous NFL and CFL teams. Gregg had a long, successful career, but succumbed to Parkinson's disease in 2019.

Alexi Grewal: Olympic gold medalist in 1984. Winning on home ground in Los Angeles, Grewal became the first American to be awarded the gold medal in the men's Olympic road race, beating Steve Bauer in a classic two up, final sprint.

Curt Harnett: former Canadian track cyclist, 3x Olympic medalist, won two silver medals at the World Track Cycling Championships and Commonwealth Games, plus eight UCI Cup medals (five gold, three silver). Harnett was the first cyclist to break the 10-second barrier in the 200 meter TT and held the world record in that event for 11 years. Was elected into Canada's Sport and Olympic Halls of Fame.

Ron Hayman: Canadian road and track racer on two Olympic teams, garnering seven National titles before turning pro, racing in Belgium, and on the iconic 7-Eleven Cycling Team. A formidable racer, he won the 1979 Tour of Ireland ahead of Phil Anderson, Stephen Roche, and Robert Millar. Won a huge prize purse at the Great Mohawk Bicycle Race, three in a row at the historic Gastown Grand Prix, and won the 1983 Tour of America. Became Men's Coach for the Canadian National Team upon retiring, mentoring the record-setting TTT squad and Olympic silver medalist Brian Walton. Hayman now hosts a training camp and stage race for juniors in the Okanagan Valley in British Columbia, Canada.

Bernard Hinault: 5x Tour de France winner (and all the classifications), three Giro GCs, and two Vuelta wins, with many stage wins en route. Renown for his ferocious racing style. Teammate Greg LeMond assisted him (and eventually rivaled him), but "Le Blaireau" (The Badger) was boss of the peloton, 1980 World Road Champion and so handsome, Peggy could hardly answer when he asked her for directions to the airport after a stage of the 1986 Colorado Coors Classic.

Bernard Hinault

Clara Honsinger: rising to the top after her first elite Cyclocross National Championship win in 2019, which upset Katie Comptom's 15-year reign and started her own. Racing in Europe, she has scored podium spots in cyclocross World Cups and won the Koppenbergcross in Belgium. Honsinger is supplementing her cyclocross with road racing at the professional level.

Hugo Houle: Canadian junior time trial National Champion in 2010, along with the road title in 2011. Won the Canadian National time trial in 2015 (and again in 2021) and in the 2015 Pan Am Games. He represented Canada in the 2016 Olympics. Competed in the Giro, the Vuelta a España, and the Tour de France, winning the Combativity award for stage 10 in the Tour de France. In 2022, Houle won the 16th stage of the Tour de France by more than a minute making him only the second Canadian rider to win an individual stage in the Tour de France, after his Israel–Premier Tech directeur sportif Steve Bauer, who won the first stage in 1988. He then followed this with second place overall at the Arctic Race in Norway. Part of Houle's motivation has been his brother who was tragically killed by a hit-and-run driver. Houle achieved his goal of winning a stage of the Tour de France solo in 2022.

Rune Hoydahl: Norwegian National Champion mountain bike racer who could win downhill or cross-country World Cups. Famous for winning five World Cups in a row in 1995. He raced in two Olympic games (1996 and 2000) representing Norway.

David "Tinker" Juarez: "Tinker" started racing BMX, turned pro, and became a founding member of the organization. In 1986, he switched to mountain bike racing, as that sport rose to prominence. He was 4x National XC Champion, won a World Cup, Pan Am gold, on two Olympic teams, and inducted into the U.S. Mountain Bike Hall of Fame. Juarez never really retired. He continues to race in masters categories and endurance events like the Race Across America, and is a 4x winner of the 24 Hour Solo Championship series.

Julien Jurdie: raced one year as a French pro and is now a directeur sportif for the AG2R Citroën team.

Jon Kabat-Zinn: molecular biologist from MIT, now teacher of mindfulness. American professor emeritus of medicine and creator of the Stress Reduction Clinic and the Center for Mindfulness in Medicine at the University of Massachusetts Medical School. He teaches mindfulness, which he says can help people cope with stress, anxiety, pain, and illness. Kabat-Zinn's stress reduction program, mindfulness-based stress reduction (MBSR), is described in his book *Full Catastrophe Living*.

David Kahl: raced BMX as a kid and cycled in high school as part of his downhill ski training. He was attending the U.S. Air Force Academy when Colorado hosted the 1986 World Championships road race and subsequently, he took up mountain bike and cyclocross. He used road cycling for cross-training which led to 2x New Jersey state 45+ Masters Road titles, a New Jersey state 50+ Elite Masters cyclocross win, and multiple 35+ and 45+ Cat 1 Masters-XC mountain bike championships.

Paul Kimmage: Irish National Champion, professional racer, and journalist most known for detailing his experiences in the book *Rough Ride*. In it, he reveals using drugs to aid his racing and talks of others' more serious drug use, creating much controversy. Kimmage interviewed Floyd Landis who admitted doping while on Lance Armstrong's U.S. Postal team. He was sued by and countersued the UCI for defamation regarding his allegations of doping in the sport.

Bobby Knight: American basketball coach "The General" is best known as the coach of the Indiana Hoosiers (1971–2000), leading them to hundreds of wins and national titles. Though volatile, he had a devoted following. After allegedly choking a player during practice, he was fired but went on to be a TV game analyst.

Clara Koppenburg: turned pro in 2015 and has a smattering of results. Nicknamed "Rambo" for her toughness, she's a natural climber, team player, and contributed to her team's 2017 TTT World Championships bronze medal.

Sepp Kuss: pro racer from Colorado. Started his career as a 3x collegiate national MTB champion (CU Boulder). Known as a climber and team player. He won a stage of the 2021 Tour de France, 10 years after the last American to win a stage, Tyler Farrar. In 2023, Kuss won the Vuelta a España, the first American to win a Grand Tour since Chris Horner won in 2013.

Atle Kvalsvoll: 6x Tour de France veteran who aided Greg LeMond in his 1990 win. Coached fellow Norwegian Thor Husvold to his 2010 World Championship title.

Peggy Maass Labiuk: *Cycle Psyched* co-author, see Labiuk's accolades under About the Authors. An innovator, she was the first U.S. track racer to use aerobars on a track bike in the 1989 National Championships, first female Provincial Cycling Coach in Canada, first to conduct indoor cycling workouts (spin classes) in B.C. While coaching World downhill champion Cindy Devine, she convinced her to warm up using a stationary trainer. They were the only ones the first year, then fighting for space on the mountain tops after that.

Steve Larsen: U.S. National Team racer, skilled in road, track, mountain bike, cyclocross, Xterra, triathlon, and Ironman. He was a

Norba National Champion in 1998 and set numerous course records blazing on the bike in triathlons. Larsen died tragically, collapsing in a workout at age 39.

Patrick Lefevere: raced professionally for just three years, culminating in winning the 4th stage in the 1978 Vuelta a España. Quickly became a top directeur sportif and has been with many variations of the Soudal Quick–Step team since its onset, the winningest team in cycling.

Greg LeMond: Won a World Road Championship in 1983. Gave Americans one of those "you remember where you were when you learned the news" moments, when he won the Tour de France in 1986. Peggy remembers being at the Olympic Training Center in Colorado Springs, cyclists yelling the exciting news. In 1987, LeMond was shot and almost killed in a hunting accident. He came back to win the Tour de France twice more, in 1989 and 1990. His career is astounding in what he accomplished, how young he was, and being the first male American to be a star in this largely European sport.

Mark Light: U.S. Masters criterium champion (age 50–54) in 2018 and Pennsylvania state road champion in 1998 are just a few of his wins in over 25 years of racing.

Jim Loehr: performance psychologist, author of 16 books. Co-founder of the Johnson & Johnson Human Performance Institute, he has researched and worked with numerous elite athletes and businesses.

Barry "Baz" Lycett: British-born, came to Canada with his set of grass track National Champion medals. Generously shared his cycling acumen with generations of cyclists, from regional level to coaching Canada's National and Olympic teams at numerous international events. Baz revived the Gastown Grand Prix race in Vancouver, making it a premier event. Now retired in Victoria, B.C., he is a recreational rider and a wonderful friend of Peggy and Saul's.

Marc Madiot: known for winning Paris–Roubaix twice (1985 and 1991) and 2x time trial stages of the Tour de France. Represented France placing 9th in the Olympics (1980) and won the Tour de l'Avenir and the National Road Championship (1987). Madiot is directeur sportif of UCI WorldTeam Groupama–FDJ.

Catherine Marsal: French cyclist who skyrocketed into stardom at a young age, winning the World Junior Road Championships and the pursuit the following year. As a senior, she won the road and TTT in 1990. She amassed multiple silver and bronze World medal performances, as well as six National Champion and 15 podium spots. Marsal won an astounding number of stages and GC titles, en route to setting the Hour Record in 1995. She represented France in four Olympics (1988, 1992, 1996, and 2000) before being hired to coach the Danish National Team.

Scott Martin: born in Colorado Springs, Colorado, sustained significant injuries as a Marine while fighting in the Iraq war. He began cycling as part of his recovery, categorized as an MC4 Paralympian. Competed in 2016 in pursuit, kilometer, road, and time trial events. He writes about cycling and was an editor of *Cycling Magazine*.

Brandon McNulty: mountain bike racer and super climber from Phoenix, Arizona, was a star as a junior before switching to road racing. A year later, he was time trial Junior National Champion. The very next year, he won the Tour de l'Abitibi, repeated the Junior National TT title, and won the junior TT World Championships. He turned pro and was second in the TT at the 2017 World Championships, bronze in 2019, still in the Under-23 category. McNulty has been noted for assisting 2021 Tour de France winner Tadej Pogačar.

Eddie Merckx: Belgian pro, "The Cannibal," is largely recognized as being the most successful racer ever. His victories include 11 Grand Tours (3x Tour de France), three World Championships, the Hour Record, 525 wins in all from 1961 to 1978. Since he raced prior to modern aerodynamic improvements, "Merckx style" is the moniker used for racing on a basic road bike.

Lori Friend Moger: owner of No Finish Line Living. A Vernon, B.C.-based kinesiologist, sport psychologist, and speaker. She earned her master's at the University of Indiana at Bloomington—you know, where *Breaking Away* was filmed. Moger helped Leah Goldstein write her memoir *No Limits* and was lead support in her Race Across America wins.

Leonard Harvey Nitz: inducted into the U.S. Cycling Hall of Fame in 1996 for his world-class performances. Harvey rode three Olympic Games—Montreal 1976, Los Angeles 1984, and Seoul 1988. In Los Angeles, he won a bronze medal in the individual pursuit and silver in the team pursuit. In the World Championships, he medaled twice in the points race—silver in 1981 and bronze in 1986. He won team pursuit gold medals in the Pan Am Games in 1983 and in 1987, adding a bronze in the kilometer time trial that year. Nitz won five National Championships in the individual pursuit (1976, 1980–1983), six in team pursuit (1980–1984, 1986) and two in the kilometer (1982 and 1984), before piling on more titles as a Masters racer.

Alex Obbard: lifelong cyclist, still blogging, and riding in the Salt Lake, Utah, area. In a 1985 *Cycling Magazine* column titled "Bike

Therapy," for which he was paid $150, Obbard described how he used cycling as a respite in a time of change in his life. In the article, he wrote that riding could almost always cheer him up and he thought it was better than seeing a shrink, as his mother suggested. Contemplating purchasing a new $2,000 bike, he figured he could justify it to his mom. He would just tell her he found a therapist, with unlimited access for a one-time fee…and his name was Gary Fisher.

Graham Obree: The "Flying Scotsman" was the great innovator of track cycling bikes and positions. He broke world records and won two World Championships (1993 and 1995) in the pursuit. The first time, he broke the world hour record (that had been held by specialist Francesco Moser for nine years), he used a narrower bottom bracket with no top tube, a one-bladed narrow fork, and straight handlebars on his "Old Faithful" bike. Obree struggled with British cycling authorities and the UCI banning his bikes and positions. Despite that, he did initiate the modern changes in bikes.

Kate O'Brien: originally a National bobsledder (2013 FIBT). Competed in 2014 for Canada, in both bobsled and cycling World Cup circuits. In 2015, Kate set a Pan Am track record in Women's Team Sprint with Monique Sullivan and a silver in individual sprint. She participated in the 2016 Olympics. A disastrous training accident in 2017 left her fighting for her life. With the help of her therapy team, Kate returned to cycling and set a new world record in C4 500-meter sprint at the UCI Para Track Championships, and then won a silver medal in the 2020 Paralympic Games in Tokyo.

John Olsen: mountain bike frame builder in the 80s in Washington state. He designed for Mercer Island Cyclery, R&E Cycles, Cannondale, and Raleigh. Olsen authored a book titled *Mountain Biking* (1990).

Connie Paraskevin: Her illustrious career began as a teen speed skater. She represented the U.S.A. at the 1984 Winter Olympics. And when cycling added the sprint event for women in the 1988 Seoul Olympics, she won bronze, having previously won four World Championship titles (1982, 1983, 1984, and 1990) and a Pan Am gold. She won ten National Championships and went to two more Olympic Games before transitioning into coaching.

Bill Parcells: The "Big Tuna" is a football coach who retired in 2007 after almost two decades of coaching pro ball. Known for turning losing teams into winners, having transformed the New York Giants (with two Super Bowl victories), the New England Patriots, New York Jets, and the Dallas Cowboys. He was welcomed into the Pro Football Hall of Fame in 2013.

Benjamin Perry: Canadian, previously a cross-country runner. A multi-time National Champion, stage winner, stage racer, recruited by Astana–Premier Tech, then with ISN. A product of the Israel Cycling Academy, Perry currently rides for UCI Continental team WiV SunGod.

Jacquie Phelan: dubbed the "Queen of Mud" in early U.S. mountain biking, co-founded NORBA (National Off-Road Bicycle Association) and won its series national title three times (1982, 1983, and 1984). She hosted the first off-road skills clinics and women's camps, started WOMBATS in 1987 (Women's Mountain Bike and Tea Society) dedicated to keeping cycling fun.

Davis Phinney: The "Cash Register" won many races and primes in the 80s and 90s, especially lucrative ones, hence the name. He was an integral part of the famous 7-Eleven Cycling Team's success and won two Tour de France stages, bronze in the TTT at the 1984 Olympics, and many races. Afflicted with Parkinson's at only 40 years old, he and (1984 Olympic gold medalist) wife Connie Carpenter use the Davis Phinney Foundation to promote living well with the disease.

Tadej Pogačar: "Youngest" seems to be the term most used to describe the Slovenian cyclist. He was the youngest to win a UCI World Tour (Tour of California) and second youngest ever to win the Tour de France. In the 2020 Tour de France, he became the only racer ever to hold three classification jerseys simultaneously: Mountains, GC, and Best Young Rider. Pogačar won Tour of Flanders, Amstel Gold, and La Flèche Wallonne classics. He won La Flèche Wallonne again in 2021. In 2023, he won a bronze medal in the World Road Race Championships.

Mary Jane Reoch: won 11 U.S. National Champion road and track titles and a World Championships pursuit silver medal (1975). "Miji" coached many cyclists and was a mentor to U.S. National Team women in Peggy's era. She was one of the first to offer private cycling coaching but was unfortunately killed during a training session by a hit-and-run driver. She was posthumously inducted into the U.S. Cycling Hall of Fame.

Gervais Rioux: Canadian National Team member in the 1988 Olympics. He now owns a bike shop and with his brother, owns the Argon 18 bike line. Rioux was inducted into the Quebec Cycling Hall of Fame.

Coryn Labecki (née Rivera): The petite sprinter (5'1") has big impact. She won 73 National titles since her start as a junior. Her breakthrough race was winning the 2017 Tour of Flanders, followed by winning the World Championships team time trial with her trade team and the 2018 U.S. Pro National Road Race Championship. She was named to the U.S. team for the Tokyo Olympic Games. Labecki won the final stage of the Giro d'Italia in 2022. Her dad raced motocross in the Philippines and mountain bikes in California. Her parents ride a tandem. She is just taking it to the next level.

Bob "Bobke" Roll: Though he did race in Europe on pro teams 7-Eleven, Motorola, and Z, "Bobke" is better known to fans as a commentator, author, and YouTuber. He raced mountain bikes, extending his competitive career with eight rides in the mountain bike World Championship. The four-time author has commentated alongside Phil Liggett and the late Paul Sherwen.

Charles Ruys: Belgian 6 Day rider of the 60s and 70s. He became a race organizer and wrote a book titled *Spotlight on 6 Day Races* in 1967. Ruys raced in the U.S. with a Dutch athlete Chris van Gent at Madison Square Garden (yes, named for track cycling's Madison), Buffalo, Chicago, Washington, DC, and Winnipeg, Manitoba.

Guy Sagiv: won the Under-23 Israeli National Road Championships in 2015, 2016, and 2019. Won the Israel Time Trial Championship in 2017 and 2020. Currently rides for ITP.

Paulo Saldanha: Race Across America participant and Ironman triathlete, this coach got Sylvan Adams into racing. His PowerWatts lab keeps tabs on upcoming Canadian cyclists and assisted Mike Woods in becoming a pro. Now performance director for the ITP Team, he coaches Woods, Froome, and Irishman Dan Martin. Saldanha is respected for his physiological and scientific knowledge and his ability to treat athletes as people—not machines.

Peter Sagan: Slovak professional cyclist, the only male cyclist to win the World Road Championships three years in a row. Sagan won the mountain bike cross-country junior World Championships in 2008 before his success on the road. In his pro career, to date he has won 115 one-day races, 14 stages in Grand Tours, and 31 of the classics.

Roger Staubach: staunch Dallas Cowboys football quarterback who was a Heisman Trophy winner, Super Bowl MVP, and named to six Pro Bowl teams. His nicknames, "Captain America," "Captain Comeback," and "Roger the Dodger," give a good idea of his reputation for pulling out victories.

Alex Stieda: the lone Canadian on the iconic 7-Eleven Cycling Team—the first American team to race the Tour de France—raced track and road and matured into a superb stage racer. His strategic solo break in the second stage of the 1986 Tour scored him enough time bonuses to hold five jerseys in total, including the polka dot as best climber, white as best rookie, red for intermediate points, and the combination jersey, in addition to the coveted yellow jersey. After losing the yellow, Stieda still held the polka dot jersey for an additional five days over the hills of northern France.

Curtis Strange: American pro golfer who was Player of the Year in 1988, topped the money list in 1985, 1987, and 1988, and the first pro golfer to earn $1 million in a single season. Won the U.S. Open two years in a row. The World Hall of Fame golfer now serves as a color commentator.

Alison Sydor: named the most successful Canadian cyclist of all times, won World Championship medals on the road and was a 3x World MTB champion (1994, 1995, and 1996). Sydor won silver in the 1992 Olympic cross-country race plus Pan Am and Commonwealth Games medals, a World Cup title, a World #1 ranking and multi-national titles to more than justify her Hall of Fame accolades.

Ricardo Ten Argiles: remarkable Spanish swimmer and cyclist who at the age of eight was severely burned and lost both arms and one leg. Argiles competed in the Paralympics (1996, 2000, 2008, 2012, 2016, and 2020), winning multiple swimming medals (in breaststroke). He took up Para cycling in 2016 and set a cycling world record in individual pursuit at the 2020 Paralympics. Watch his Paralympic ride at https://www.facebook.com/reel/50341635600 26989/.

Geraint Thomas: started with success on the velodrome with world records and titles in team pursuit along with Olympic golds (2008 and 2012). Switching to the road, he advanced from being a time trial specialist, to support rider and leadout man, to winning the Tour de France overall (2018), winning the famed Alpe d'Huez stage while wearing the yellow jersey. In 2023, he was race leader in the Giro d'Italia but finished second overall before securing 3rd place overall in the Tour de France.

Joe Tosi: coach and, according to David Ryan in the Hartford Courant, "the majordomo of bike racing" in the 70s. He died tragically when hit by a truck while riding his bike. David Ertl, who wrote *101 Cycling Workouts*, was coached and mentored by Tosi when he started racing in Connecticut and viewed him as "a coach before there were coaches."

Larry Towner: winner of 20 New Jersey state titles in cyclocross, road, time trail, and track. Always liked the science end of coaching and was an early adopter of heart rate monitors.

Sven Tuft: Canadian time trial National Champion (2004–2006). Had a colorful background and career start in British Columbia and worked his way up to a silver medal ride in the 2008 World Championships time trial. Who knows, if he hadn't flatted in the final 5 km, he may have won gold. He also won silver in the TTT in the 2014 World Championships and was well respected by teammates and fellow racers.

Cecilie Uttrup Ludwig: 3x Danish time trial National Champion. Uttrup Ludwig is the winner of the Tour of Scandinavia (2022) and the Giro dell'Emilia Internazionale Donne Elite (2020). She won a stage in the Tour de France Femmes (2022), placed 2nd in La Flèche Wallonne Féminine (2020) and in La Course by Le Tour de France (2021). Her bronze medal in the 2023 Pro Women's Road Race at the World Championships marks her place on the world stage.

Nelson Vails: "The Cheetah" from New York City was a bike messenger on a single speed. Won gold in the sprint at the 1983 Pan Am Games and silver in the 1984 Olympic Games. He paired with Les Barczewski on the tandem to sprint to silver in the 1985 World Championships, and won four National titles. He had a role in the film *Quicksilver* with Kevin Bacon (1986) and did TV commentary. You can ride with Vails as he makes appearances at Gran Fondos.

Jennifer Valente: one of the winningest American track stars. Valente has five UCI World Championship titles, capturing a total of 10 World Championship medals in six different events. Her greatest accomplishment was becoming the Olympic champion at the Tokyo Olympic Games (2020) in the women's omnium event.

Wout van Aert: Belgian, won cyclocross World titles (2016, 2017, and 2018). Accumulated 9x Tour de France stage wins, classic wins Amstel Gold, 2x E3 Saxo classic, Milano–San Remo, Strade Bianche, Gent–Wevelgem, Omloop Het Nieuwsblad ME, five stages in the Critérium du Dauphiné, the Tour of Britain GC, as well as the Points GC in the Tour de France (2022) and the Tour de Suisse (2023). Van Aert added a Road World Championships silver medal to his count. He is a versatile racer and team support rider on the Jumbo–Visma squad.

Jean-Paul "Popeye" van Poppel: Dutch road sprinter who won multiple stages in all three Grand Tours from 1985–1994. He was the first high-profile former pro to manage a pro women's team. (*Peggy*: "I was in awe to be around him when I was coaching the British National Women's Team, and astonished that the racers didn't seem to know "Popeye" as a famous pro racer.")

Annemiek van Vleuten: retired at age 40 at the top of her career. She has won World Championships 2x road race, 2x time trial, Olympic gold in time trial (2016), silver in road race (2020), 4x Dutch road and time trial National Championships, 5x Giro Donne, Tour de France Femmes (2022), 3x La Vuelta Feminina, 6x Grand Tours, and was the first woman to complete both the Giro and the Tour in the same year. The 3x Dutch Woman of the Year is considered one of the greatest female cyclists ever.

Jonathan Vaughters: was 1997 U.S. time trial National Champion before being signed to the U.S. Postal Team with Lance Armstrong. His career was marred by crashes and injuries which prevented him from finishing his four Tour de France starts, but he was part of the team winning the TTT in 2001. He also admitted to drug use and converted to speaking out against its use in sport. In 2003, he started a junior team in Colorado, then co-founded Slipstream Sports in 2005, based on his belief that there was a better way to run a cycling team. Vaughters launched an American pro Tour team by 2009, which participated in the Tour de France and Giro d'Italia. He was elected president of the International Association of Professional Cycling Groups. His Garmin–Cervélo squad took the top position in the team classification in the Tour de France (2011). As a staunch defender of ethical competition and fair play, he heads the EF–Education—now

EF Education First Drapac p/b Cannondale—identifying and coaching riders while managing the overall operations of the team.

Demi Vollering: won the Liège–Bastogne–Liège Femmes (2021), her first win in a major classic. In 2023, she won all three Ardennes classics—the Amstel Gold Race, La Flèche Wallonne Féminine, and Liège–Bastogne–Liège Femmes. She won the Dutch National Road Championship (2023), beginning the path to her victory in the Tour de France Femmes, and recently added the overall win in the Tour de Romandie Féminine and the World Road Championships silver medal to complete her season.

Brian Walton: His career spanned 18 years. He participated in three Olympic Games, winning a silver medal in the points race in Atlanta (1996). He started as a road racer and was introduced to track, unlike many who start out on the track and progress to the road. Walton won Britain's prestigious Milk Race in 1989 and amassed 10 Canadian national titles before turning to coaching and founding his own business, Walton Endurance in Atlanta, specializing in customized corporate cycling events.

Felicity "Flick" Wardlaw: Australian road racer (2013–2015). Won the National TT in 2014.

Paul "Wolf" Willerton: former pro, raced with Greg LeMond as a domestique and supported Lance Armstrong in the 1992 World Championships. Disillusioned, Willerton switched to mountain bike racing for his penultimate 1994 season and placed 6th in the World Championships XC race. When Armstrong's doping was finally revealed in 2012, he protested Nike's continued sponsorship of Armstrong, picketing in front of their headquarters. It was successful in pressuring them to drop the support. Willerton is part owner of DeFeet cycling socks company.

Justin Williams: Following in his Belizian father's footsteps, he began racing as a teen and won numerous junior national titles on the track. As a senior, he won keirin, criterium, and the Under-23 Road Race titles, and was picked up by the U.S. National Team. While racing in Europe, he supported Taylor Phinney in his 2010 Paris–Roubaix Espoirs race win. Returning to the U.S., he raced for various teams and won the U.S. National criterium and road race in 2018, repeating the amateur road title in 2019 and 2021. Williams created Team L39ION, working to increase inclusion and innovation in cycling, and mentoring Black and Hispanic riders. Williams just launched the CRIT circuit racing series.

Russell Wilson: NFL All-Pro quarterback, spent 10 seasons with the Seattle Seahawks before joining the Denver Broncos. Wilson holds the record for most wins by an NFL quarterback through his first nine seasons, and won an NFL Super Bowl championship.

Eric Wolberg: Canadian Cycling Hall of Fame Wolberg represented Canada in three Olympics (1996, 2000, and 2004) and won gold at the 1998 Commonwealth Games TT, adding a bronze in the road race. He also won gold in the time trial in the 1999 Pan Am Games, the same year he won the famous Tour of Somerville (and repeated in 2001). He accumulated eight time trial National Championships, won the Tour de Beauce, 2x Tour de Hokkaido, 2x Hotter'N Hell 100, Tour of the Gila, 2x the Cat's Hill Classic, Fitchburg Longsjo Classic, Nevada City Classic, Tour de Nez, Tour of Wellington, as well as numerous stage wins over his 13-year career. Now a directeur sportif for Human Powered Health.

Michael Woods: world-class runner turned cyclist. Athleticism propelled him to a World Championship bronze medal in the 2018 pro road race. Woods is the only professional who has run a sub four-minute mile and also competed in the Tour de France. His late start in cycling made him one of the oldest neo pros in the sport. 2019 saw him win Milano–Torino. Representing Canada in the Tokyo Olympics, he placed 5th in the road race. He held the red king of the mountains jersey in the Tour de Suisse and the polka dot climber's jersey in the 2021 Tour de France, and won stage 9 of the 2023 Tour de France.

Roger Young: former speed skater, Olympic track sprinter (1972), U.S. National sprint champion (1973), team pursuit bronze in the Pan Am Games (1975). Young is part of the U.S.A. cycling royalty, he is brother-in-law to Jim Ochowicz (directeur sportif of 7-Eleven, Motorola, BMC, and himself a former Olympian), and was married to cyclist Connie Paraskevin. He won the Tour of Somerville in 1972 and coached top sprinters Connie Paraskevin and Canadian Curt Harnett.

ACKNOWLEDGMENTS

We wish to acknowledge the following individuals whose contribution made the book possible. First, those athletes and sport support people we consulted with personally, either while coaching with them or directly in the development of *Cycle Psyched*: Sylvan Adams, Alex Amiri, Houshang Amiri, Vic Armijo, Erin Attwell, Marie-Claude Audet, Steve Bauer, Cassie Campbell, Micaiah Besler, Ray Cipollini, Brendan Cleak, Marion Clignet, Maggie Coles-Lyster, Nicole Cooke, Richard DeGarmo, David Ertl, Kevin Field, Jakub Fisher, Chris Froome, Zack Garland, David Gaudu, Leah Goldstein, Shaul Gordon, Ron Hayman, Phoebe Haymes, Curt Harnett, Clara Honsinger, Hugo Houle, David Kahl, Mark Light, Barry Lycett, Lori Friend Moger, Shaima Nasiri, Alex Obbard, Damian O'Hagan, John Pierce, Benjamin Perry, Gervais Rioux, Guy Sagiv, Paulo Saldanha, Alex Stieda, Larry Towner, Sven Tuft, Nelson Vails, Alexey Vermeulen, Shelley Versus, Brian Walton, Renate Walton, and Eric Wohlberg. Also supporters and friends: Lesley Beatson, Dennis Labiuk, Donald Maass, Garfield Lindsay Miller, Barbara Pappas, and the Wenzel Coaching group, especially Kendra Wenzel and Paul Page-Hanson.

We wish to acknowledge the following individuals whose insights we gleaned from their media comments: Kristen Armstrong, Edward "Eddie B" Borysewicz, Mark Cavendish, Steve Cook, Calvin Coolidge, Fausto Coppi, Larson Craddock, Alessandro De Marchi,

Chloe Dygart, Albert Einstein, Jakob Fuglsang, Phil Gaimon, Felice Gimondi, Missy Giove, Forest Gregg, Alexi Grewal, Bernard Hinault, Rune Hoydahl, Fabio Jacobsen, Tinker Juarez, Julien Jurdie, Jon Kabat-Zinn, Paul Kimmage, Bobby Knight, Clara Koppenburg, Sepp Kuss, Atle Kvalsvoll, Steve Larsen, Patrick Lefevere, Greg LeMond, Marc Madiot, Catherine Marsal, Scott Martin, Brandon McNulty, Eddie Merckx, Leonard Harvey Nitz, Alex Obbard, Graham Obree, Kate O'Brien, John Olsen, Bill Parcells, Jacquie Phelan, Davis Phinney, Tadej Pogačar, Mary Jane Reoch, Coryn Rivera, Bob Roll, Charles Ruys, Peter Sagan, Roger Staubach, Curtis Strange, Alison Sydor, Ricardo Ten Argiles, Geraint Thomas, Joe Tosi, Cecilie Uttrup Ludwig, Wout van Aert, Jean-Paul van Poppel, Annemiek van Vleuten, Jennifer Valente, Jonathan Vaughters, Jonas Vingegaard, Demi Vollering, Felicity Wardlaw, Paul Willerton, Justin Williams, Russell Wilson, Michael Woods, Connie Paraskevin, Roger Young.

We would also like to acknowledge and thank Laara K. Maxwell for her editorial acumen and the team at Spring Cedars Publishing, especially Audrey Zurcher for her insight, creativity, and editorial expertise.

NOTES

Introduction

[1] Nicole Cooke: personal communication with Peggy Maass Labiuk

[2] Steve Bauer: personal communication with Dr. Saul Miller and Peggy Maass Labiuk

[3] Lenard Harvey Nitz: Bill Strickland, *The Quotable Cyclist*, Breakaway Books, 2001

[4] Peter Sagan: Martin Fraas, "You Have to Do Your Own Thing," *Bora*, March 2021, https://www.bora.com/int/en/you-have-to-do-your-own-thing/

Chapter 1

[5] Alexi Grewal: Bill Strickland, *The Quotable Cyclist*, Breakaway Books, 2001

Chapter 2

[6] Alison Sydor: Dr. Saul Miller and Peggy Maass Hill, *Sport Psychology for Cyclists*, Velopress, 1999

[7] Leah Goldstein: personal communication with Dr. Saul Miller

[8] Tadej Pogačar: Velon, "Tour de France 2020: Retro Tadej Pogačar," *YouTube*, September 21, 2020, https://www.youtube.com/watch?v=yD5i0q7yIiE

[9] Phil Gaimon: Phil Gaimon, *Draft Animals*, Penguin Books, 2017

[10] Chris Froome: personal communication with Dr. Saul Miller

[11] Alex Stieda: personal communication with Dr. Saul Miller

[12] Michael Woods: PowerWatts International, "Coffee Shop Talks with Paulo Saldanha," *Facebook*, April 19, 2020, https://www.facebook.com/watch/?v=220423619055226

[13] Sylvan Adams: personal communication with Dr. Saul Miller

[14] Mark Light: personal communication with Peggy Maass Labiuk

[15] Peggy Maass Labiuk

Chapter 3

[16] Michael Woods: PowerWatts International, "Coffee Shop Talks with Paulo Saldanha," *Facebook*, April 19, 2020, https://www.facebook.com/watch/?v=220423619055226

[17] Jonathan Vaughters: Netflix, "Tour de France: Unchained," composed by Dan Caplin, June 8, 2023

[18] Tinker Juarez: Bill Strickland, *The Quotable Cyclist*, Breakaway Books, 2001

[19] David Kahl: personal communication with Peggy Maass Labiuk

[20] Geraint Thomas: Netflix, "Tour de France: Unchained," composed by Dan Caplin, June 8, 2023

[21] Chris Froome: personal communication with Dr. Saul Miller

[22] Guy Sagiv: personal communication with Dr. Saul Miller

[23] Marie-Claude Audet: personal communication with Dr. Saul Miller

[24] Larry Towner: personal communication with Peggy Maass Labiuk

[25] Jennifer Valente: Velo.OutsideOnline.com, "Olympic track cycling: Jennifer Valente wins Omnium gold," August 7, 2021, https://velo.outsideonline.com/road/road-racing/olympic-track-cycling-jennifer-valente-wins-omnium-gold-kelsey-mitchell-gold-for-canada-in-the-sprint/

[26] Connie Paraskevin: Bill Strickland, *The Quotable Cyclist*, Breakaway Books, 2001

[27] Missy Giove: Bill Strickland, *The Quotable Cyclist*, Breakaway Books, 2001

Chapter 4

[28] Albert Einstein: Bill Strickland, *The Quotable Cyclist*, Breakaway Books, 2001

[29] Jacquie Phelan: Bill Strickland, *The Quotable Cyclist*, Breakaway Books, 2001

[30] Joe Tosi: Bill Strickland, *The Quotable Cyclist*, Breakaway Books, 2001

[31] Paul Willerton: Bill Strickland, *The Quotable Cyclist*, Breakaway Books, 2001

[32] Peggy Maass Labiuk

[33] John Olsen: Bill Strickland, *The Quotable Cyclist*, Breakaway Books, 2001

[34] Nelson Vails: personal communication with Dr. Saul Miller

[35] Patrick Lefevere: Netflix, "Tour de France: Unchained," composed by Dan Caplin, June 8, 2023

[36] Brian Holm: Netflix, "Tour de France: Unchained," composed by Dan Caplin, June 8, 2023

[37] Chris Froome: personal communication with Dr. Saul Miller

[38] Erin Attwell: personal communication with Peggy Maass Labiuk

[39] Larry Towner: personal communication with Peggy Maass Labiuk

Chapter 5

[40] Demi Vollering: Lyne Lamoureux, "Demi Vollering Wins the Tour de France Femmes 2023," *CyclingNews.com*, July 30, 2023, https://www.cyclingnews.com/races/tour-de-france-femmes-2023/stage-8/results/

[41] Paulo Saldanha: personal communication with Dr. Saul Miller

[42] David Gaudu: Netflix, "Tour de France: Unchained," composed by Dan Caplin, June 8, 2023

[43] Chris Froome: personal communication with Dr. Saul Miller

[44] Felice Gimondi: Bill Strickland, *The Quotable Cyclist*, Breakaway Books, 2001

[45] Brian Walton: personal communication with Dr. Saul Miller

[46] Curtis Strange: *Quote Fancy*, www.quotefancy.com/quote/1619136/curtis-stange

[47] Benjamin Perry: personal communication with Dr. Saul Miller

Chapter 6

[48] Annemiek van Vleuten: Shane Stokes, "Smiling in final farewell: Annemiek van Vleuten shrugs off misfortune in swan song world champs," *Velo.OutsideOnline.com*, August 16, 2023, https://velo.outsideonline.com/road/road-racing/smiling-in-final-farewell-annemiek-van-vleuten-shrugs-off-misfortune-in-final-world-champs/

[49] Cassie Campbell: personal communication with Saul

[50] Greg LeMond: Bill Strickland, *The Quotable Cyclist*, Breakaway Books, 2001

[51] Hugo Houle: personal communication with Dr. Saul Miller

[52] Coryn Labecki: Riley Missel, "Coryn Rivera (Finally!) Wins the US Professional Road Cycling Championships," *Bicycling.com*, June 27, 2018, https://www.bicycling.com/racing/a21969787/coryn-rivera-finally-wins-the-us-professional-road-cycling-championship/

[53] Erin Attwell: personal communication with Peggy Maass Labiuk

[54] Alex Amiri: personal communication with Peggy Maass Labiuk

[55] Eric Wolberg: personal communication with with Dr. Saul Miller

[56] Bob Roll: BobkeTV, "Worst Bike Throws in Cycling," *YouTube*, October 7, 2016, https://www.youtube.com/watch?v=MFHvjYBQxiU

[57] Greg LeMond: Bill Strickland, *The Quotable Cyclist*, Breakaway Books, 2001

[58] Wout van Aert: Netflix, "Tour de France: Unchained," composed by Dan Caplin, June 8, 2023

[59] Marc Madiot: Netflix, "Tour de France: Unchained," composed by Dan Caplin, June 8, 2023

[60] Scott Martin: Bill Strickland, *The Quotable Cyclist*, Breakaway Books, 2001

[61] Catherine Marsal: Giles Belbin, "A life in cycling: Catherine Marsal," *CyclingNews.com*, March 8, 2021, https://www.cyclingnews.com/features/a-life-in-cycling-catherine-marsal/

[62] Ron Hayman: personal communication with Dr. Saul Miller

[63] Sean Kelly: Richard Windsor, "Taking the pain: What does it mean to suffer," *Cycling Weekly*, October 23, 2017, https://www.cyclingweekly.com/fitness/training/what-does-it-mean-to-suffer-356111

[64] Felicity Warlaw: Richard Windsor, "Taking the pain: What does it mean to suffer," *Cycling Weekly*, October 23, 2017, https://www.cyclingweekly.com/fitness/training/what-does-it-mean-to-suffer-356111

[65] Geraint Thomas: Netflix, "Tour de France: Unchained," composed by Dan Caplin, June 8, 2023

Chapter 7

[66] Julien Jurdie: Netflix, "Tour de France: Unchained," composed by Dan Caplin, June 8, 2023

[67] Eddie Merckx: Bill Strickland, *The Quotable Cyclist*, Breakaway Books, 2001

[68] Leah Goldstein: personal communication with Peggy Maass Labiuk

[69] Steve Bauer: personal communication with Dr. Saul Miller

[70] Sylvan Adams: personal communication with Dr. Saul Miller

[71] Sepp Kuss: Cycling Pro Net, "Sepp Kuss - post-race interview - Stage 15 - Vuelta a España 2019," *YouTube*, September 15, 2019, www.youtube.com/watch?v=v7SWCkuqWEw

[72] Forest Gregg: Howard Ferguson, *The Edge*, Getting The Edge Co, 1990

[73] Leah Goldstein: communication with Dr. Saul Miller and Peggy Maass Labiuk

[74] Leah Goldstein: communication with Dr. Saul Miller and Peggy Maass Labiuk

[75] Steve Larsen: Bill Strickland, *The Quotable Cyclist*, Breakaway Books, 2001

[76] Chris Froome: Chris Froome, "Training on Teneride," *YouTube*, March 13, 2021, www.youtube.com/watch?v=W07pzuTzH1Y

[77] Justin Williams: Jonny Long, "US road champion Justin Williams: Being in a sport that is primarily white it was hard not to feel alone, it broke me," *Cycling Weekly*, June 3, 2019, https://www.cyclingweekly.com/news/latest-news/us-road-champion-justin-williams-sport-primarily-white-hard-not-feel-alone-broke-425990

[78] Julian Alaphilippe: Alasdair Fotheringham, "Julian Alaphilippe to balance pressure to perform with enjoying second season as world champion," *Cycling Weekly*, January 11, 2022, https://www.cyclingnews.com/news/julian-alaphilippe-to-balance-pressure-to-perform-with-enjoying-second-season-as-world-champion/

[79] Wout van Aert: Netflix, "Tour de France: Unchained," composed by Dan Caplin, June 8, 2023

[80] Jakob Fuglsang: Mary Cárdenas, "CyclingPub interview - Jakob Fuglsang: To look for something new at 34 is a big risk," *CyclingPub.com*, January 7, 2020, http://cyclingpub.com/article/6923/

[81] Calvin Coolidge: Howard Ferguson, *The Edge*, Getting The Edge Co, 1990

[82] Benjamin Perry: personal communication with Dr. Saul Miller

[83] Paul Kimmage: Paul Kimmage, *Rough Ride*, Yellow Jersey Press, 1990

[84] Rune Hoydahl: Bill Strickland, *The Quotable Cyclist*, Breakaway Books, 2001

[85] Mark Madiot: Netflix, "Tour de France: Unchained," composed by Dan Caplin, June 8, 2023

[86] Marion Clignet: personal communication with Peggy Maass Labiuk

[87] Marion Clignet: "Inspirational Epilepsy Stories: Marion Clignet," *Epsy*, September 18, 2020, https://www.epsyhealth.com/seizure-epilepsy-blog/inspirational-epilepsy-stories-marion-

[88] Marion Clignet: personal communication with Peggy Maass Labiuk

[89] Marion Clignet: "Inspirational Epilepsy Stories: Marion Clignet," *Epsy*, September 18, 2020, https://www.epsyhealth.com/seizure-epilepsy-blog/inspirational-epilepsy-stories-marion-

[90] Alex Stieda: personal communication with Dr. Saul Miller

[91] Barry Lycett: personal communication with Dr. Saul Miller

[92] Maggie Coles-Lister: Maggie Coles-Lister, "Re-Defining Resilience," *MaggieColesLister.com*, May 16, 2020, https://www.maggiecoleslyster.com/post/re-defining-resilience

[93] Bobby Knight: Howard Ferguson, *The Edge*, Getting The Edge Co, 1990

[94] Eddie B Borysewicz: Bill Strickland, *The Quotable Cyclist*, Breakaway Books, 2001

[95] Charles Ruys: Bill Strickland, *The Quotable Cyclist*, Breakaway Books, 2001

[96] David Gaudu, Netflix, "Tour de France: Unchained," composed by Dan Caplin, June 8, 2023

[97] Larson Craddock: "Craddock's career-lows motivate for future races," *NBCSports.com*, July 7, 2020, https://www.nbcsports.com/video/lawson-craddock-finds-motivation-despite-not-racing-2019-tour-de-france

[98] Graham Obree: Bill Strickland, *The Quotable Cyclist*, Breakaway Books, 2001

Chapter 8

[99] Davis Phinney: Bill Strickland, *The Quotable Cyclist*, Breakaway Books, 2001

[100] Marc Madiot, Netflix, "Tour de France: Unchained," composed by Dan Caplin, June 8, 2023

[101] Chloe Dygert: "Voxwomen Cycling Podcast p/b Brother UK: Chloe Dygert," *Voxwomen*, May 18, 2020, https://voxwomen.com/i-go-into-every-race-thinking-im-going-to-win-in-conversation-with-chloe-dygert/

[102] Chloe Dygert: John Croom, “Chloe Dygert talks UCI Worlds TT and the 2020 Olympic Games Coffee and Van Chats Podcast,” *YouTube*, June 19, 2020, https://www.youtube.com/watch?v=bewvXQZ6UHE

[103] Nelson Vails: personal communication with Peggy Maass Labiuk

[104] Russell Wilson: “Seahawks Daily—Separation is in the Preparation,” *Seahawks.com*, https://www.seahawks.com/video/seahawks-daily-separation-is-in-the-preparation-146616

[105] Clara Honsinger, personal communication with Peggy Maass Labiuk

[106] Bill Parcells: Howard Ferguson, *The Edge*, Getting The Edge Co, 1990

[107] Roger Staubach: Howard Ferguson, *The Edge*, Getting The Edge Co, 1990

[108] Greg LeMond: Bill Strickland, *The Quotable Cyclist*, Breakaway Books, 2001

[109] Jean-Paul van Poppel: Bill Strickland, *The Quotable Cyclist*, Breakaway Books, 2001

[110] Marc Madiot: Netflix, “Tour de France: Unchained,” composed by Dan Caplin, June 8, 2023

Chapter 9

[111] Maggie Coles-Lyster: personal communication with Dr. Saul Miller

[112] Socrates

[113] Clara Koppenburg: “CyclingPub Interview - Clara Koppenburg: I can be one of the best climbers if I believe in myself,” *CyclingPub.com*, April 18, 2019, http://cyclingpub.com/article/5653/

[114] Atle Kvalsvoll: Bill Strickland, *The Quotable Cyclist*, Breakaway Books, 2001

[115] Mary Jane Roach: Bill Strickland, *The Quotable Cyclist*, Breakaway Books, 2001

[116] Hugo Houle: personal communication with Dr. Saul Miller

[117] Gervais Rioux: personal communication with Dr. Saul Miller

[118] Bernard Hinault: Bill Strickland, *The Quotable Cyclist*, Breakaway Books, 2001

[119] Phil Gaimon: Phil Gaimon, *Ask a Pro*, VeloPress, 2017

[120] Chloe Dygert: John Croom, “Chloe Dygert talks UCI Worlds TT and the 2020 Olympic Games Coffee and Van Chats Podcast,” *YouTube*, June 19, 2020, https://www.youtube.com/watch?v=bewvXQZ6UHE

[121] Anna Kiessenhofer: “What the stars said after Anna Kiessenhofer derailed the Dutch with Olympic triumph,” *Velo.OutsideOnline.com*, July 25, 2021, https://velo.outsideonline.com/road/road-racing/what-the-stars-said-after-anna-kiesenhofer-derailed-the-dutch-with-olympic-triumph/

[122] Sven Tuft: personal communication with Dr. Saul Miller

[123] Kevin Field: personal communication with Dr. Saul Miller

[124] Brandon McNulty: Philippe Tremblay, "Rally-UHC teamwork key to Brandon McNulty's Giro di Sicilia win," *Canadian Cycling Magazine*, April 7, 2019, https://cyclingmagazine.ca/sections/news/rally-uhc-teamwork-key-to-brandon-mcnultys-giro-di-sicilia-win/

[125] Sylvan Adams, personal communication with Dr. Saul Miller

[126] Alessandro De Marchi: Barry Ryan, "De Marchi: My way of doing things is more romantic than modern cycling allows," *CyclingNews.com*, May 11, 2021, https://www.cyclingnews.com/news/de-marchi-my-way-of-doing-things-is-more-romantic-than-modern-cycling-allows/

[127] Chris Froome: personal communication with Dr. Saul Miller

[128] Kristen Armstrong: Kristin Frattini, "Kristin Armstrong: Chloe Dygert's crash is devastating but she will come back stronger," *CyclingNews.com*, September 24, 2020, https://www.cyclingnews.com/news/kristin-armstrong-chloe-dygerts-crash-is-devastating-but-she-will-come-back-stronger/

[129] Coryn Labecki: Riley Missel, "Coryn Rivera (Finally!) Wins the US Professional Road Cycling Championships" *Bicycling.com*, June 27, 2018, https://www.bicycling.com/racing/a21969787/coryn-rivera-finally-wins-the-us-professional-road-cycling-championship/

[130] Steve Cook: Bill Strickland, *The Quotable Cyclist*, Breakaway Books, 2001

[131] Alex Obbard: Bill Strickland, *The Quotable Cyclist*, Breakaway Books, 2001

[132] Greg LeMond: Bill Strickland, *The Quotable Cyclist*, Breakaway Books, 2001

[133] Peter Sagan: Martin Fraas, "You Have to Do Your Own Thing," *Bora*, March 2021, https://www.bora.com/int/en/you-have-to-do-your-own-thing/

[134] Chris Froome: personal communication with Dr. Saul Miller

[135] Jim Loehr: James E. Loehr, *Mental Toughness Training for Sports*, Stephen Greene Press, 1986

[136] Ricardo Ten Argiles: *Kurere*, https://www.kurere.org/historias/ricardo-ten?widget=1

[137] Kate O'Brien: Aishwarya Kumar, "Former Olympian Kate O'Brien wins silver medal in cycling at Tokyo Paralympics," *ESPN.com*, August 27, 2021, https://www.espn.com/olympics/story/_/id/32097126/former-olympian-kate-obrien-wins-silver-medal-cycling-tokyo-paralympics

[138] Greg LeMond: BrainyQuote, https://www.brainyquote.com/quotes/greg_lemond_158834

[139] Fausto Coppi: "A cycling transformation in Rome," *Union Cycliste Internationale*, July 16, 2020, https://www.uci.org/article/a-cycling-transformation-in-rome/7u8JSXD8BEt8TV5pL62EgR. Original quote by Robert Strauss.

Lifestyle

[140] Albert Einstein: *BrainyQuote*, https://www.brainyquote.com/quotes/albert_einstein_737829

141 Cecilie Uttrup Ludwig: Laura Weislo, “Women’s World Championship medalists open up about mental stress in cycling,” *CyclingNews.com*, August 13, 2023, https://www.cyclingnews.com/news/womens-world-championship-medalists-open-up-about-mental-stress-in-cycling/

142 Hugo Houle: personal communication with Dr. Saul Miller

143 Demi Vollering: Lyne Lamoureux, “Demi Vollering Wins the Tour de France Femmes 2023,” *CyclingNews.com*, July 31, 2023,

144 Clara Honsinger: personal communication with Peggy Maass Labiuk

145 Shaul Gordon: personal communication with Dr. Saul Miller

146 Barry Lycett: personal communication with Dr. Saul Miller

147 Phil Gaimon: Phil Gaimon, “Former Pro Cyclist Phil Gaimon Has a New Goal: Finding the Best Cookies in America,” *SportsIllustrated.com*, Auguist 14, 2017, https://www.si.com/eats/2017/08/14/phil-gaimon-best-cookies-cycling

148 Jakub Fisher: personal communication with Dr. Saul Miller

149 Brandon McNulty, Edmond Hood, “PEZ Talk: UAE’s Brandon McNulty,” *Pez Cycling News*, April 16, 2020, https://pezcyclingnews.com/interviews/pez-talk-uae-team-emirates-brandon-mcnulty-rider-interview/

150 Roger Young: Bill Strickland, *The Quotable Cyclist*, Breakaway Books, 2001

151 Jon Kabot-Zinn: Myla and Jon Kabay-Zinn, *Everyday Blessings*, Hachette Books, 1998

152 Peter Sagan: Martin Fraas, “You Have to Do Your Own Thing,” *Bora*, March 2021, https://www.bora.com/int/en/you-have-to-do-your-own-thing/

153 Mark Cavendish: Netflix, “Mark Cavendish: Never Enough,” directed by Alex Kiehl, July 25, 2023

154 Leah Goldstein: communication with Dr. Saul Miller and Peggy Maass Labiuk

155 Lori Friend Moger: personal communication with Dr. Saul Miller

156 Nelson Vails: personal communication with Dr. Saul Miller and Peggy Maass Labiuk

157 Jonas Vingegaard: Netflix, “Tour de France: Unchained,” composed by Dan Caplin, June 8, 2023

158 Fabio Jakobsen: Netflix, “Tour de France: Unchained,” composed by Dan Caplin, June 8, 2023

Contributors

159 Mark Cavendish: Netflix, “Mark Cavendish: Never Enough,” directed by Alex Kiehl, July 25, 2023

Made in the USA
Columbia, SC
19 December 2024